高校英语选修课系列教材

EFFECTIVE WORKPLACE ENGLISH WRITING

职场英语写作

主 编 陈 洁
编 者 陈 洁
　　　　廖海宏

清华大学出版社
北 京

内 容 简 介

《职场英语写作》内容涉及简历、求职信、商业信件、备忘录、邮件、会议议程与纪要、执行摘要、提案报告、调查报告、口头汇报、网页设计与写作等十余种在各行业中使用频率较高、要求严格、覆盖面广的体裁形式。编者遵照讲授知识、训练能力、内化素质、推动实践的构思，组织素材和优化内容，旨在帮助读者获得当代企事业管理、商业运作和现代办公所需的英语交流与写作技能，增强职业素养，提升职场竞争力。

版权所有，侵权必究。举报：010-62782989，beiqinquan@tup.tsinghua.edu.cn。

图书在版编目（CIP）数据

职场英语写作 / 陈洁主编. —北京：清华大学出版社，2022.8
高校英语选修课系列教材
ISBN 978-7-302-61313-8

Ⅰ.①职…　Ⅱ.①陈…　Ⅲ.①英语—写作—高等学校—教材　Ⅳ.① H319.36

中国版本图书馆 CIP 数据核字（2022）第 122344 号

责任编辑：白周兵
封面设计：子　一
责任校对：王凤芝
责任印制：沈　露

出版发行：清华大学出版社
　　　　　网　　址：http://www.tup.com.cn, http://www.wqbook.com
　　　　　地　　址：北京清华大学学研大厦 A 座　　邮　编：100084
　　　　　社 总 机：010-83470000　　邮　购：010-62786544
　　　　　投稿与读者服务：010-62776969, c-service@tup.tsinghua.edu.cn
　　　　　质量反馈：010-62772015, zhiliang@tup.tsinghua.edu.cn
　　　　　课件下载：http://www.tup.com.cn, 010-83470410

印 装 者：三河市铭诚印务有限公司
经　　销：全国新华书店
开　　本：185mm×260mm　　印　张：15.75　　字　数：318 千字
版　　次：2022 年 8 月第 1 版　　　　　　　印　次：2022 年 8 月第 1 次印刷
定　　价：68.00 元

产品编号：091872-01

前言

无论你是一名即将步入职场的学生，还是一名拥有多年工作经验的员工，掌握简洁、准确、及时、有效的沟通技能，都是推进职业生涯、通往事业成功的先决条件。工作中，沟通的形式多种多样，其中有很大一部分是书面交流。很多用人单位都会将良好的写作技能列为考核新员工和现任员工的重要标准。

《职场英语写作》从当代企事业管理、商业运作和现代办公的需要出发，解决即将步入职场的青年学生或职场人士在英语写作方面的技能训练和能力培养问题。通过突出"知识+能力+素养+实践"的主体架构，精心组织内容，帮助读者从巩固英语书面交流的基础知识出发，逐步获得工作中所需要的写作技能，切实提升书面交流能力，增强职业素养，达成表达自如、沟通顺畅、能够解决实际工作问题的预期目标。同时，注重创新思辨能力与家国情怀、国际视野的培养。

本教材共八章，包括 Introduction、Language Techniques for Effective Writing、Document Design、Writing for Job Opportunities、Basic Correspondence、Reports、Writing for the Oral Presentation 和 Writing for the Web。在讲授英语写作基础知识和电脑写作技术的同时，编者将敏锐的触角延伸到包括简历、求职信、商业信件、备忘录、邮件、会议议程与纪要、执行摘要、提案报告、调查报告、口头汇报、网页设计与写作等十余种在各行业中使用频率较高、要求严格、覆盖面广的体裁形式。每章均有配套练习，由编者精心编写和反复打磨而成，供读者检验学习效果，提高实战能力。

本教材是湖南省一流本科课程"实用英语写作"的衍生，课程建设获得了中南大学"创新创业教育课程建设"立项，教材建设获得了"中南大学本科教材项目"立项。教材的编写与出版依托教育部产学合作协同育人项目"新文科建设背景下高校实用英语写作课程建设改革与实践"，并深入贯彻其精神。本教材的部分内容已经在中南大学英语专业（"国家一流专业"）的教学中使用多年，希望能在未来的"新文科"教育教学改革实践中，为培养"新文科"复合型创新人才和高素质涉外人才发挥积极作用。

本教材适合本科院校和大专院校在校学生及有意提升职场竞争力的人士使用。

鉴于时间仓促和编者水平有限，本教材难免有疏漏和不足之处，欢迎广大读者批评指正。

陈洁

2022 年 5 月

Contents

Chapter 1   Introduction 1

     1.1   The Value of Effective Writing at Work 2

     1.2   Characteristics of Work-related Writing 5

     1.3   Phases of Writing 8

Chapter 2   Language Techniques for Effective Writing ... 15

     2.1   You-attitude 16

     2.2   Seven Cs 20

     2.3   Active Voice Versus Passive Voice 35

     2.4   Positive and Unbiased Tones 36

     2.5   Punctuation 40

Chapter 3   Document Design 49

     3.1   The Importance of Good Document Design 50

     3.2   Choosing Typefaces Carefully 51

     3.3   Using "Chunking" to Communicate 54

     3.4   Creating Good Headings 55

     3.5   Using a Good Layout for Columns and Lists 58

     3.6   Using Block Paragraphing and White Space Effectively 63

     3.7   Incorporating Visuals 66

Chapter 4 — Writing for Job Opportunities 73

- 4.1 Highlighting Reader-centered Communication 74
- 4.2 Marketing Yourself as a Job Seeker 77
- 4.3 Résumés 80
- 4.4 Cover Letters 96

Chapter 5 — Basic Correspondence 105

- 5.1 Writing Persuasive Messages 106
- 5.2 Conveying Good News, Neutral News, and Bad News 110
- 5.3 Business Letters 114
- 5.4 Memos 128
- 5.5 Emails 141

Chapter 6 — Reports 153

- 6.1 Report Types 154
- 6.2 Report Components 156
- 6.3 Procedures of Creating Reports 159
- 6.4 Meeting Minutes and Agendas 168
- 6.5 Executive Summaries 173
- 6.6 Proposal Reports 176
- 6.7 Surveys 183

Chapter 7 Writing for the Oral Presentation 187

- 7.1 Understanding the Oral Presentation as a Way of Communication 188
- 7.2 Preparing an Audience-targeted Oral Presentation ... 192
- 7.3 Making an Audience-targeted Oral Presentation 205

Chapter 8 Writing for the Web 211

- 8.1 Differences Between a Web Page and a Website 212
- 8.2 Major Types of Websites Used in the Workplace 214
- 8.3 Processes of Creating Reader-centered Web Pages 223
- 8.4 Skills in Developing Content-based Web Pages 225

References 231

Keys to Exercises 233

Chapter 1
Introduction

The ability to concisely and accurately convey meaning to different people is a prerequisite in today's fast-paced world. Whether you are a student about to step into the workplace or a more seasoned employee with years of experience, you must be able to communicate effectively to advance your career. You communicate in many ways at work. A large amount of this communication is in writing. Some employers consistently rank good writing skills—whether the document is printed or on the screen—among the desired skills for both new hires and current employees.

In this chapter, you will learn about:

- the value of effective writing at work;
- characteristics of work-related writing;
- phases of writing.

1.1 The Value of Effective Writing at Work

In a working environment, when would you choose to communicate through writing? Typically, you will choose to communicate through writing when one or more of the following conditions are in place:

- A permanent document is required.
- The intended receiver of the message is not present.
- The sender of the message wants to establish a formal interaction with the receiver.

At work in administration, business or management, and in any other profession, you probably use a pen and a computer keyboard more than any other equipment. Writing is one thing that you must do every day, and success in your career depends largely on your ability to express your thoughts clearly, simply, and persuasively in your writing. However, many people enter the workplace clueless about the right way to frame a request or compose a routine email. They may wonder about some issues, such as how the document should look like, what tone to adopt, or which organizational strategy to use. Learning how to write professionally begins with the awareness of the value of effective writing at work. Exactly speaking, the value of effective writing at work is as follows.

Chapter 1 Introduction

1.1.1 The Place of Writing at Work

Writing is important to work. Estimates of the time people spend writing in a normal workday run upwards of 25%. If we also count both the time spent planning writing and the time spent reading what others have written, the figure is close to 40%. That is a lot of time, and it represents a significant work expense.

Poor writing is bad work. It slows down the communication process, causes confusion, and encourages mistakes. Most workplaces are inundated with paperwork for too many papers around—reports are too long, memos too frequent, correspondence too burdensome. When the writing is not only lengthy but bad—filled with mistakes, poorly organized, unclear—it becomes a hindrance rather than a tool for work.

But good writing is more than just a tool for work. Let's take business as an example. In the widely heralded information economy era, written information (whether in hard copy or electronic form) is often the commodity that is being traded. Product documentation, feasibility studies, product brochures, test reports—these all represent business products just as manufactured goods do.

1.1.2 The Role of Individual Writing in the Workplace

Good writing is also important at the individual level. Writing serves to establish and maintain an employee's role within a company. The impressions made on you as a worker, especially by higher-ups who are not in your immediate work setting, are often based on what you write.

The memos and reports that employees write also serve as a primary means of individual evaluation. No one may ever say outright that you will be evaluated on your written reports or memos, but all too frequently nobody knows what you did until you put it in writing. Thus writing serves as a key means of job evaluation and plays a large role in decisions concerning promotions and merit rises.

Many employees do not define writing as their work. They say they are test engineers, or biologists, or sales representatives, or accountants. Yet these workers spend much of their time writing, and many of their work activities are directly aimed at producing some written products. Writing is a tool closely related to success within the organization; the higher they move up within an organization, the more important and time-consuming writing becomes.

1.1.3　The Merits of Effective Writing at Work

Help You to Concentrate

Preparing a description, like making a careful drawing or preparing a plan to scale, makes you concentrate on the object or event to be described and helps you to ensure that your record is both accurate and complete. Similarly, entering observations on a data sheet during any practical investigation or inquiry, with words or numbers, makes you concentrate on your work and helps you to ensure that each entry is inserted at the right time—so that all necessary data are recorded.

Help You to Remember

The ability to listen, select, and make concise notes relevant to your present or possible future needs is an important skill at work. In administration, business, and management, you make notes during conversations, interviews, and meetings, so that you can remember:

- the subject discussed (a heading);
- with whom it was discussed;
- when it was discussed (the date);
- the gist of what was said (a few words, phrases, numbers and dates, and complete sentences where necessary);
- any conclusions and anything agreed on.

Help You to Think

In writing, you capture your thoughts. Writing is therefore a creative process that helps you to sort your ideas and preserve them for later consideration. Preparing a memo or a report makes you set down what you know, and so leads you to a deeper understanding of your work. For example, preparing a progress report helps you to view an aspect of your work as a whole, to recognize gaps in your knowledge, to avoid time-wasting distractions, and to know when the work is complete.

Help You to Be Well-organized and Time-effective

Making a note of the things you expect to complete is of much help. You may also find it helpful to work to some kind of weekly timetable, which may be on a page, on which you can enter firm commitments and notes of things you hope to achieve at other times. Even if you cannot plan each week in detail, your list of the things you plan to do each day is the basis of efficient organization. For example:

- Prepare the list as you decide what needs to be done.
- Number the tasks as you decide your order of priority.
- Cross tasks off your list as they are completed, and add new tasks as they are brought to your attention.
- Revise your order of priority as new tasks are added to the list.

By working to a job list each day or weekly or monthly, you develop a good habit of effective time management. This not only makes for efficiency but also helps you to avoid stress by being in control, which can benefit you in the long run.

1.2 Characteristics of Work-related Writing

Workplace writing has certain characteristics that form the underpinning of anything you write, from an email to your boss, to a résumé for a new job, to a proposal for a new business. When you think of work-related writing, what characteristics come to your mind?

At first, you typically write work-related documents for a specific audience/reader and the work-related documents should be useful to the audience/reader. Then, they should be well-organized, clear, concise, accurate, and complete. Many work-related documents contain visuals, such as graphs, diagrams, or tables, even pictures. Last but not least, the tone of work-related writing tends to be more objective and unbiased; it also attempts to maintain a positive tone.

All in all, remember to integrate the following characteristics into your writing at work.

Accuracy

Professionalism comes first in the workplace. One of the best ways to illustrate to our readers that we are professionals and experts is through accuracy. Inaccuracy shows carelessness that few professionals or organizations can afford in a competitive, global marketplace.

Brevity

Brevity is expected in workplace communication. No one wants to wade through wordy prose to get to a point. Conciseness in work-related writing can save time and effort, thus enhancing communication efficiency.

Clarity

If a reader has to reread to understand anything you write, it means that you have not done your job well. Every sentence you write should be easy to read. Clarity comes from using words the readers will recognize and use correctly. Stay away from unnecessary jargon or technical terms. One way to check your work for clarity is to give your draft to someone who knows nothing about what you are writing. If he or she can understand the document, it is probably clear.

Correctness

Poor grammar and word use make both the writer and the organization appear ignorant and sloppy. To hone your grammatical skills, work with a grammar guide next to you. Consult the guide when you are unsure about any writing issue. Make good use of your word processor's grammar and spelling check, but do not rely on them solely.

Strong Nouns and Verbs

Good writing uses nouns and verbs to do the heavy work and saves adverbs and adjectives for rare occasions. Instead of "Our auto policies are competitive", say "Our auto policies beat the competitor's". Be cautious about the overuse of *is*, *are*, *was*, and *were*, for "be" is regarded as the most boring and overused verb in the English language. On the one hand, "be" is a weak verb form, in part because it indicates a state of existing rather than action. Furthermore, "be" verbs are sort of passive rather than active.

Simple Words

Avoid jargon and choose the simpler, more recognizable word over the longer, more flowery one. Instead of *rhinovirus*, use *a cold*. Opt for *email* over *electronic message*. In *utilize* versus *use*, *use* wins. Just imagine how the number of words your reader has to wade through goes down with simpler words or everyday language.

Chapter 1 Introduction

Sentence Variety

Sentence variety has two elements. The first is sentence beginnings. It means to avoid writing sentences that begin with the same word or phrase. As you edit, look at the way your sentences begin. Do three sentences in a row begin with *I*? Or do two sentences within one paragraph begin with *There are*? Make your sentence beginnings different and attractive. The second way to attain sentence variety is to vary the sentence length. Natural-sounding prose combines short, medium, and longer sentences. We have several ways to alter the sentence lengths. Join two sentences whose content is closely linked by embedding the gist of one sentence into the other. Combine two sentences with a coordinate conjunction to make a complex sentence. Or try an alternate sentence beginning, such as an introductory phrase, which will add sentence variety.

Parallelism

Good writing often uses a device called parallelism, or parallel structure. Writers use parallelism instinctually because it appeals to our natural desire for symmetry. Parallelism matches nouns with nouns, verbs with verbs, and phrases with phrases as in "I came, I saw, I conquered." Readers expect parallelism, especially in sets of two or three items, and in bulleted or enumerated lists. Using parallel phrasing correctly is key to effective writing in the workplace.

Shorter Paragraphs

Big blocks of type scare readers away. Long paragraphs are appropriate for essays, but they have no place in professional documents. In work-related writing, the longest ideal paragraph should be no more than six to eight lines. Always be aware of how a paragraph appears on a page (or a screen), and take pity on your readers—don't make them slog through dense prose.

Positive Voice

Cultivate a positive image for you and your organization. A positive voice uses affirmative words to make a point. For example, instead of saying "We are out of blue shoes", you would emphasize the positive and say "Order any size of our white and black shoes". Avoid downbeat words or words that can convey a negative connotation and rephrase them positively. Instead of "No coupons will be honored after May 1", say "Coupons will be honored through May 1".

Appropriate Level of Formality

Whether to use an informal or formal writing style depends on the reader and the purpose of the document. There is no clear-cut way to determine when to use each style. Most of the time, emails are informal. However, sometimes, an email may require formality. To determine which style fits your needs, understand that informal writing allows you and the reader to connect at a more personal level. It can convey closeness, warmth, and friendliness. Formal writing, on the other hand, produces the impression of objectivity, seriousness, and professionalism.

Table 1.1 can help to guide you in choosing which style best suits your writing task.

Table 1.1 Comparison between formal style and informal style

	Types of Documents	Characteristics
Formal style	Letters Long reports Research proposals	No personal pronouns (*I*, *we*, etc.) No contractions Objective voice or use of passive voice No figurative language or clichés No editorializing Limited use of adjectives No exclamation points Longer sentences Some technical language
Informal style	Most communication within the organization including emails, memos, text messages Routine messages to outside audiences Informal reports	Use of personal pronouns Use of contractions Shorter sentences Easily recognizable words Limited use of warm, inoffensive humor

1.3 Phases of Writing

You should use a systematic process to develop your written documents. Every composition, whether it is a short business letter, an essay written by a student, an article in a magazine, a set of instructions, or a long report, should be undertaken in three phases. The process of writing can be described with an acronym: AWE, short for *assess*, *write*, and *evaluate*. The following will illustrate the three phases of work-related writing.

Phase 1: Assess

This phase includes the following steps:

- Analyze the audience.
- Identify the purpose.
- Gather information.
- Organize the information.

Before you ever put pen to paper or put your fingers on the keyboard, begin by assessing the writing situation and defining your readers and purpose.

Knowing the audience—your reader—is imperative for successful writing. As a writer, if you can put yourself in your reader's shoes, you will establish a mutually successful relationship, and your correspondence will be well received. Your reader will feel comfortable building a relationship with you, and you will have earned that reader's trust, loyalty, and most definitely his or her business or cooperation. This applies to clients, colleagues, supervisors, and subordinates—everyone. Consider first the needs of the people you expect to read any communication you are preparing. What are their backgrounds? What are their interests? What do you think they have already known about the subject of your composition? Writers need to be very clear about the target audience because the language and style we use depend upon who will read what we write. In essence, we have to psych out the reader to accomplish our writing goal. Written communication is more than the transfer of a message. Unless the message makes sense to the intended reader, that reader cannot respond properly and the communication is not effective. Here are some things you should determine about your reader:

- Is the reader technical or non-technical?
- How will the reader use this information?
- What are his or her expectations?
- What is his or her current knowledge on this topic?
- What kind of reader is he or she?

These are just examples of questions that will help you to understand your reader. As you build your professional relationships, you will be able to dig into even finer details about your reader that will personalize and enhance your communication.

The next part of assessing the writing situation is defining your purpose. Knowing your purpose keeps you focused. The purposes of most work-related writing fall into three basic categories: informing, persuading, and requesting.

- Informative writing is a large category that includes generalized information, instructions, notifications, warnings, or clarifications.
- Persuasive writing makes an impression, influences decisions, gains acceptance, sells goods, or makes recommendations.
- Requests are written to gain information or rights and to stimulate action.

Once you have defined for whom you are writing and what you want to accomplish, continue your analysis of the writing situation by gathering the information to produce the document. Sometimes you may just need to extract information from your experience. Sometimes you need to conduct research. Sometimes you need to turn to the internet. This step is named information gathering. Anyhow, have your information on hand before you begin to write.

Once you have the information, organize it. You will need to decide how you want to organize your material to present it to the reader. A useful organizational tool is an outline which, whether formal or informal, is essentially a list of your major topics and subtopics in the sequence in which you want to present them. For example, you can add numbers to your notes as you decide:

1. What is the main point to be made in each paragraph?
2. How should you begin?
3. In what order should the other paragraphs follow?
4. What explanation or examples must be included in each paragraph?
5. Are there any tables or diagrams needed?
6. If there are, where should they be placed?
7. How should you end?

By adding numbers to indicate the order of paragraphs, you convert your first thoughts into a plan or topic outline. Preparing this plan will serve to remind you of relevant things that you already know, and to recognize gaps in your knowledge or information.

Phase 2: Write

This phase includes the following two steps:

Chapter 1 Introduction

- Create the first draft.
- Revise the draft yourself.

A draft by definition is not final. Enter the first step of the writing process—writing a draft—knowing that it is not the last step. Its purpose is to transfer the information you have gathered onto the page. For short documents, such as routine emails, consider composing offline. (It's too tempting to write and hit "send" without carefully going over your draft.) Begin by including the information you've gathered, making sure you include each point. For longer documents, use your outline. With your ready outline as a guide, you can write with the whole composition in mind—with each word contributing to the sentence, each sentence to the paragraph, and each paragraph to the composition, and with meaning as the thread running through the whole. Knowing how you will introduce the subject, the order of paragraphs, and how you will end, you will be able to:

- begin well;
- avoid repetition by dealing with each topic fully in one paragraph;
- ensure relevance;
- emphasize your main points;
- include comment and connecting words to help your readers along;
- write quickly, maintaining the momentum that makes a composition hold together;
- arrive at an effective conclusion.

Write section by section, and point by point. If you have trouble with one section, move to another. Your goal at this phase of writing is to put something down on paper (or the screen) that you will revise later. Don't worry too much about the mechanics, such as spelling, grammar, punctuation, sentence structure, paragraphing, and transitioning between paragraphs. Remember, in the first-draft phase, the important thing is to get those ideas down.

Check your work, therefore, and revise it carefully so that your readers do not have to waste time trying to understand an uncorrected first draft that reflects neither your intentions nor your ability. Before you move to the next step, print your draft for revision. If you have been working on a computer screen, you are advised to print out your first draft so that you can see several pages at once, if necessary, as you can check the whole document. But don't read it immediately. When you have finished the first draft, the best thing you can do is get away from it for a while, for as long as it is comfortable for you. This time away clears your mind and allows you to look at the material with fresh eyes and mind. When you return, revise your draft for the mechanics mentioned above, and the following questions should be kept in your mind as well:

- Does your first draft read well?
- Is it well-balanced?
- Are the main points sufficiently emphasized?
- Is anything essential missing?
- Is the meaning of each sentence clear and correct?
- Does the writing match the needs of your readers, in vocabulary, sentence length, and style?

Revision is a means of improving the first draft, but if enough thought has been given to thinking and planning before writing, there should not be many mistakes with the first draft. In administration, business, and management, people may not have time to write everything twice; revision is most likely to be necessary for preparing long documents that cannot be completed in one sitting. Please remember that the revised document is the best product you can produce yourself. Do your best!

Phase 3: Evaluate

Getting independent feedback is crucial in the phase of evaluation.

To admit that you need to revise your early drafts and that you can benefit from a colleague's constructive comments and suggestions or an editor's advice is not to say that you are unintelligent. Even after several revisions, you may not appreciate all the difficulties of a reader. Other people coming fresh to your composition may suggest improvements. It is a good idea, therefore, to ask at least two people to read your corrected draft of any important document that is other than routine. They may see things that are not sufficiently explained, words that are irrelevant, unnecessary, or out of place, and sentences that are ambiguous or do not convey the meaning they think you intended to. They may draw your attention to mistakes, badly presented arguments, and good points that require more emphasis.

Many times, people want to skip this phase. They think that once they revise the draft, they can distribute the document to their readers. However, what you should do at this point is get an independent review of your document. Here are some basic questions to have the reviewer answer:

- Does this make sense?
- Am I being clear?
- Is there anything confusing?

The independent review can be informal "eyeballing" of the document by a colleague. Some organizations conduct a formal review of documents, such as instructions and procedures, in which formal problem reports are submitted to the writer. Since the quality of your writing at work reflects on your employer as well as on yourself, some employers have a procedure for editing and revising important documents. Your employer may also wish to ensure that nothing confidential or classified as a secret is reported.

》Exercise

Study the following extracts from compositions written by people who were presumably trying to do their best work. Try to detect faults in the extracts respectively.

Extract 1

Safe and efficient driving is a matter of living up to the psychological laws of motion in a spatial field. The driver's field of safe travel and his minimum stopping zone must accord with the objective possibilities, and a ratio greater than unity must be maintained between them. This is the basic principle. High speed, slippery road, night driving, sharp curves, heavy traffic, and the like are dangerous, when they are, because they lower the field zone ratio.

Extract 2

Without guidance or instruction, skill is acquired by making a series of attempts until a sense of familiarity or mental and physical economy or achievement, suggests that a particular attempt is directed towards the desired goal. That this way of learning can be uneconomical of time and indeed often unsuccessful is demonstrated, for example, by two-finger typists who, even though they work quickly, do not achieve the speed and accuracy of their correctly trained counterparts.

Chapter 2
Language Techniques for Effective Writing

Your purpose in any workplace communication depends on your audience and the occasion. You should try to amuse, convince, inform, instruct, persuade, or sympathize with your audience. Whatever you do, your intention should always be both to be understood and to affect other people in a chosen way. This chapter provides you with language techniques that enable you to communicate more effectively in your writing. The more you remember to incorporate these techniques, the more effective your workplace writing will be. Your message will be easier for the reader, your audience, to interpret and understand.

In this chapter, you will learn about:

- you-attitude;
- seven Cs;
- active voice versus passive voice;
- positive and unbiased tones;
- punctuation.

2.1 You-attitude

2.1.1 What Is You-attitude?

"You-attitude" is a word used by Kitty O. Locker in *Business and Administrative Communication*, which refers to a style of writing that puts readers' needs first. Specifically, you-attitude emphasizes what readers want to know, respecting their intelligence, and protecting their ego.

Locker details five strategies for achieving you-attitude in writing. (1) Talk about the reader, not about yourself. (2) Refer to the reader's request or order specifically. (3) Don't talk about feelings, except to congratulate or offer sympathy. In most professional settings and situations, your feelings are irrelevant. (4) Use "you" more often than "I" in positive situations. Doing so accentuates the good news associated with the reader. (5) Avoid the word "you" in delivering bad news, as it can be interpreted as accusatory and over-accentuate the negative.

In workplace writing, it is important to focus on the reader, that is, to "talk" to the reader. This means emphasizing "you", either implicitly or explicitly, in your writing. Why do you want to achieve this you-attitude? Readers tend to pay more attention if they are spoken to. Also, it communicates respect for the readers and empathy for the readers' viewpoints. It also tends to focus on your readers' interests, desires, and preferences. If your message emphasizes "I" or "we", then you can appear to be uninterested in your readers.

Using the you-attitude in your writing implies that you are focusing on your readers and appreciate their viewpoints. Here are some examples of the appropriate use of the you-attitude.

Table 2.1 Examples of you-attitude expressions

Original Version	You-attitude Revision
To enable us to process your order, we require a 20% down payment.	Your order requires a 20% down payment.
We are pleased to provide you with 24-hour access to your account.	You now have 24-hour access to your account.

Of course, in some instances, you should avoid emphasizing "you". In a negative situation, such as when you mention bad news or correct a mistake, you typically will not use "you", to avoid placing blame. If your company prefers a more formal, distant style, confine your use of "you" to informal documents, such as letters and memos.

Table 2.2 Examples of avoiding emphasizing "you"

Instead of Using	Use
You must get approval from your supervisor before you leave your production area.	Employees must obtain their supervisor's approval before leaving their production area.
You should never use that procedure to release this valve.	That procedure doesn't work to release this valve.

2.1.2 Writing from the Reader's Point of View

When you are writing at work, on most occasions, you are writing to communicate with your readers and persuade them to take action and thus achieve your purpose. To persuade your readers, you need to make your readers perceive you as a trustworthy person and convince them to believe that their interests and benefits will be served and your ideas, plans, products, services, etc. are practical and will cater to their needs if accepted. Try to empathize with your readers and ask yourself what they want or need to know. Rather than focus on yourself, your request, acclaim, service, or product, stress your readers' needs and their benefits if they comply with your message. For example, no matter how talented, versatile, and capable you are, when you are writing to apply for a certain job, you must understand your prospective employer's needs and try to analyze his or her possible reactions to the information you offered in your cover letter and résumé, and select appropriate education background and experience catering to the employer's needs and convince him or her that you are qualified for the opening position.

You-attitude writing strategies applied in writing cover letters and résumés will make the reader or employer give you the opportunity for an interview. In some instances, you-attitude in correspondence writing is an important persuasive strategy helping you to move on smoothly with your work and greatly enhance work efficiency, for example, to convince your manager to agree with your creative engineering design or your business proposal, or to encourage your business partner to sign a contract or an agreement for a certain profitable project.

The following is an example of memo writing with you-attitude:

MEMORANDUM

To: Evan Crisp
From: Xavier dela Cruz (XD)
Date: February 26, 2021
Subject: Best Practices for Communication Between Professors and Students

Effective communication involves conveying the topic or issue with professionalism, urgency, and consideration. The items listed below are recommended guidelines that can elicit a prompt response by your addressee:

- **Proper use of grammar and spelling** will convey professionalism and emphasize the urgency of any issues that need to be addressed. Avoid the use of colloquialisms, jargon, or slang since it may cause misunderstanding.
- **Entering a clear and succinct subject line** will prepare your reader for the topics that are contained within the email. Consider your addressee, and provide concise details on the subject.

Chapter 2 Language Techniques for Effective Writing

(Continued)

- **Promptly respond to any replies or questions** by the addressee. This will let your addressee know that you value his or her time.
- **Demonstrate enthusiasm for** the course by elaborating on its significance on your university and career plans.
- **End the email with proper information**, such as your contact information and an expression of gratitude to your addressee.

By following these aforementioned guidelines, you are conveying urgency on your issue while remaining considerate towards your addressee. If you have any questions, you can email me at student@alumni.ubc.ca.

2.1.3 Putting Yourself in the Reader's Place

Business letters, memos, and emails with a message based on the perspective of "me" usually neglect the reader's self-interest, and thus will create a distance for the social and business relationship. You-attitude helps you to cope with the problem and will make your reader be willing to read your message and feel being cared for after reading the message, thus forging a stronger social or business relationship especially when you are writing to readers who are not pleased, interested, or willing to take action before reading your correspondence.

In order to convince your readers not only to accept your message mentioned in the business letters, memos, or emails, but also to accept your presentation of ideas, to take action on the request, or to make an adjustment based on your request in the writing, you need to have a specific purpose to write with you-attitude.

One of the writing strategies is to establish a good, respectful relationship with your readers by addressing them directly in your correspondence and start with "you" "your" or "yours", not just the first person "I" "me" "mine" "we" "us" or "ours". Write in the active voice with a courteous, tactful, and gracious touch of language. This is fully illustrated in Table 2.3.

Table 2.3 Examples of sentences with and without you-attitude

Without You-attitude	With You-attitude
In order to complete our inventory early, we will be closing early on February 10, please come to shop early on that day.	We invite you to shop at our supermarket early on February 10 so we can meet your needs before our early closing at 6 p.m. so as to complete our inventory early.
We are Moonlight Travel Agency. Please believe our services can help you to become a happy traveler.	You'll enjoy a happy journey in the city by staying with a well-trained team of Moonlight Travel Agency.
We have requested that your order be sent out next Monday.	You will receive your order by next Thursday.
We offer a tour guide service.	You can now book our tour guide service for sightseeing in the city online at your convenience.

2.2 Seven Cs

The seven Cs are a checklist of the qualities of good professional and business communication that you should apply to your workplace writing. Good professional and business writing are clear, concise, concrete, complete, courteous, coherent, and constructive. Although we will illustrate the seven Cs one by one in the following, these seven principles overlap quite a bit. A sentence that is not complete will also be less clear, coherent, and courteous.

2.2.1 Clear

If you want to get your message across, the best thing you can do is get to the point. Say what you want to say, support it with facts, be specific, ask for what you need, thank the reader, and then end the letter. Another word for "clear" is "transparent". Good writing is transparent: The readers never ever have to go back over a sentence or paragraph to puzzle out what the writer meant because the material is always clearly and logically presented.

There are six basic ways to achieve the goal of being clear.

Avoid Jargon and Technical Terms or Obscure Words

How about "eponymous", a word that occasionally appears in writing for the general

Chapter 2 Language Techniques for Effective Writing

public? Is "eponymous" part of most readers' vocabularies? Probably not. An "eponymous" hero is one whose name is the title of a work, such as Tom Sawyer. Most readers don't want to consult the dictionary every few paragraphs just because a fancy word (like "eponymous") makes the writer appear intelligent. As for jargon, technical terms, and the like, if you have to use them, then you must also define them unless you are sure your readers are completely familiar with these terms.

Use Active Verbs

An active verb has the subject of the sentence doing the action, as in "Tom [subject] ate [action] two hamburgers [object]." The natural or default order for an English sentence is the doer [subject] and what he or she or it did [verb], then the object [what Tom ate, in this example]. The verb here should be an active verb.

Most of the time you should use active words except when:
- you want to introduce variety in sentence structure;
- the doer of the action isn't precisely known (e.g. "Eight thousand students have been admitted to Central South University this year.");
- the doer of the action isn't as important as the action itself (e.g. "Interest rates were raised half a point last week.").

In such cases, we turn to the passive voice flexibly.

Avoid Strings of Prepositional Phrases

Prepositions are short (usually) linking words, such as *in*, *on*, *with*, *over*, and so on, which begin prepositional phrases. Look at an example:

> The results *of* the physics experiment tests *of* the students *at* Central South University were excellent.

The above sentence has three prepositional phrases. Any sentence with a long string of prepositional phrases could be called a word salad; the sentence's meaning gets buried in a jumble of unnecessary words. The sentence can be rewritten to reduce the number of prepositional phrases from three to one:

> Student physics experiment test results *at* Central South University were excellent.

Note that most prepositional phrases can be turned into words that function as adjectives (by modifying or describing nouns). In the example above, instead of "The results *of* the...tests", you can write "...test results".

Make Pronoun References Crystal Clear

Look at this sentence:

➢ The manager asked his executive assistant to finish the report before *he* left for the day.

To whom does the pronoun "he" refer? The meaning of the sentence is not clear because the pronoun reference "he" is not clear.

Pronouns are place-keeper words; they stand in for (the Latin "pro" means "for") nouns. As a writer, you must make sure that, if you use a pronoun as a place keeper, readers never ever have to puzzle over who or what that pronoun refers to. The grammar term for this problem, by the way, is the unclear pronoun reference. If in doubt, repeat the noun:

➢ The manager asked his executive assistant to finish the report before the assistant left for the day.

Please check the following sentence carefully to see if there is any problem.

➢ Each cabinet member must be responsible for the security of *their* briefcase.

Those who reject this usage, called the singular "they", argue that the pronoun ("their") is plural, but the noun the pronoun refers to ("member") is singular. In grammar, this problem is called faulty noun-pronoun number agreement, abbreviated as NPNA. The rule is that pronouns must always agree in number—singular or plural—with the nouns they refer to. What about this fix?

To avoid using the singular "they", you have three options:

- making the noun plural ("Cabinet members must be responsible for the security of their briefcases.");
- making the pronoun singular ("Each cabinet member must be responsible for the security of his or her briefcase.");
- taking out the pronoun entirely ("Briefcase security is every cabinet member's responsibility.").

Avoid Dangling and Misplaced Modifiers

A dangling modifier is a word or phrase that modifies (gives additional information about) a subject that doesn't exist in the sentence. For example:

> Flying into Seattle, the mountains were beautiful.

What the sentence intends to mean is that "we" thought the mountains were beautiful as we flew into Seattle, but "we", the subject, is missing, who is "flying into Seattle". The fix for this dangling modifier is to add a proper subject, a noun that could be in an airplane admiring the view:

> Flying into Seattle, *the passengers* thought the mountains were beautiful.

A misplaced modifier is a word or phrase that appears to modify the wrong noun, because it is poorly placed in the sentence. For example:

> I have a book written by William Shakespeare in my office.

William Shakespeare didn't write the book in the speaker's office because he's long dead. Therefore, "in my office" is a misplaced modifier. Instead, the sentence should read:

> In my office, I have a book written by William Shakespeare. / I have in my office a book written by William Shakespeare.

The fix for a misplaced modifier is to move it closer to, and preferably next to, the noun or pronoun it modifies.

Avoid Hedge Words and Phrases

Hedge words and phrases are used when the writer is looking for a buffer to soften his or her statement. It is usually done because he or she is either not prepared to submit something as fact, or thinks he or she can dodge the issue by hiding it in extra words. Here are some common hedge words and phrases in Table 2.4 that you should avoid when writing.

Table 2.4 Hedge words and phrases

according to our records	if I recall	likely
as far as I can tell	in due time	might
as per your request	in my humble opinion	mostly
as you might know	in the near future	permit me to say
could	in view of	probably
for your information	it is my understanding that	pursuant to
I wish to thank	just about	with reference to

2.2.2 Concise

Some of the best-written works of all time have been clear and concise. Conciseness and clarity go together. The more concise a piece of writing, the more likely it is to be clear. The following guidelines (some are the same as for clear writing) will make your writing more concise.

Use Active Verbs

Please note that the active verb structure also uses fewer words than the passive structure (which includes added words, usually a form of the verb "be"). For example:

- Tom *ate* two hamburgers.
- Two hamburgers *were eaten* by Tom.

The active sentence has four words, while the passive sentence has six. Active verbs are, therefore, not only clearer than passive verbs but also more concise.

In karate training, students are told that their fists must be tightly clenched when they throw a punch; if the fist isn't tight, the bones of the hand will break. The same is true of writing; tight, concise writing is punchy, powerful writing.

Avoid the Verb "Be" Whenever Possible

"Be" is a weak verb form, and it is often unnecessary. "Be" verbs are usually found in the passive forms of verbs. Make the verb active and "be" verbs usually disappear. For example:

- The meeting is going to *be attended* by teachers in the English Department next week.
- English teachers *will attend* the meeting next week.

On the conciseness index, that's 8 words compared to 15.

Sometimes even active sentences can fall into the "be" trap. For example:

- The tact is *of much help* to the housewives.
- The tact *helps* the housewives much.

That's 6 words instead of 9. The wordy construction in this example is called nominalization which will be mentioned later; and how to avoid nominalization is another key to brevity.

"Be" constructions, such as "there is" "there are" and "it is" can also almost always be trimmed.

> *There are* five ducks in the pond. = Five ducks *are* in the pond.

Even better:

> Five ducks *splashed* in the pond. (a more dynamic active verb)

Similarly, "It is easy to jump rope." is less concise and punchy than "Jumping rope is easy."

Avoid Nominalization

Nominalization occurs when you use a verb or other parts of speech as a noun. Nominalization weakens your writing and makes your sentences less concise. For example:

> The teacher *made the comment* that the class has made great progress this term.

The "comment" is the noun form of the verb "comment". So why not cut to the chase and use the verb alone for a much more concise and punchy sentence?

> The teacher *commented* that the class has made great progress this term.

That's 12 words instead of 14.

Table 2.5 shows examples of avoiding nominalization.

Table 2.5　Examples of avoiding nominalization

Instead of Using	Use
They have the effect of making your sentences less concise.	They make your sentences less concise.
Huawei asked the managers to make a decision about the new sales promotion campaign.	Huawei asked the managers to decide on a new sales promotion campaign.

Avoid Long Strings of Prepositions

Any sentence with a long string of prepositional phrases can be rewritten to reduce the number of prepositional phrases. For example, more than three modifiers before the noun they modify create a word salad, and you need to reintroduce a prepositional phrase or two. We have discussed avoiding prepositional word salads in the "2.2.1 Clear" part.

Chisel Away Needless Words

One of the most overused and unnecessary phrases in the English language is "in order to". For example:

> In order to submit the report before the deadline, we need to work overnight.

How about the simpler "To submit the report before the deadline, we need to work overnight."? The second sentence means the same thing, and you've gotten rid of two words—"in order"—that do no useful work whatsoever.

Table 2.6 offers some examples of wordy phrases, along with some options.

Table 2.6 Examples of wordy phrases and concise alternatives

Wordy Phrases	Concise Alternatives
a great deal of	much
at all times	always
do an analysis of	analyze
in order to	to
in the course of	during
in the event that	if
make a recommendation	recommend
subsequent to	after
the majority of the time	usually/frequently
until the time when	until
with regard to	regarding
with the exception of	except

Avoid Redundancy

While sometimes it is important to repeat ideas to get your message understood, be careful not to overdo it. There is a difference between effective repetition and redundancy. Use repetition as a tool only when it helps to emphasize your point. Table 2.7 has a list of redundant phrases and their more crisp alternatives:

Table 2.7 Examples of redundant phrases and concise alternatives

Redundant Phrases	Concise Alternatives
collectively assemble	assemble
continue on	continue
contractual agreement	contract/agreement
cooperate together	cooperate

Chapter 2 Language Techniques for Effective Writing

(Continued)

Redundant Phrases	Concise Alternatives
current status	status
endorse on the back	endorse
final completion	completion
final outcome	outcome
first priority	priority
foreign imports	imports
invisible to the eye	invisible
normal practice	normal/practice
other alternatives	alternatives
refer back	refer
repeat again	repeat
revert back	revert
true facts	facts
tuition fees	tuition
whether or not	whether
vitally important	important

A variation of redundancy is "go without saying", or GWS. GWS refers to words, phrases, or sentences that are so obvious that they don't need to be said. Here is an example of GWS:

➢ Visual aids make the website attractive for the viewer.

If the website is attractive, that implies a viewer, so you don't need to mention the "viewer". The following is a table to give some examples of GWS:

Table 2.8   Examples of GWS

GWS	
absolutely	in other words
actually	in the end
basically	in the final analysis
currently	last but not least
as a matter of fact	the fact of the matter is
at this moment in time	in view of the fact that
in due course	to all intents and purposes

2.2.3 Concrete

Concrete words appeal to the senses—they describe things we can see, hear, feel, smell, or touch, thereby painting a vivid mental picture. No writing technique is more powerful than being concrete and specific. For example:

> Congressman Robin Williams made an exciting speech in the House of Representatives yesterday.

What does this tell us, concretely and specifically, about Williams' speech? Nothing. We don't even know what he spoke about. If Williams made an exciting speech, then the writer should be concrete and specific about what Williams said and what made his speech exciting. For example:

> Slamming his fist on his desk, face red with outrage, Congressman Robin Williams condemned the Independence Day parade shooting in Chicago.

Please note that the more concrete and specific a piece of writing is, the clearer it is as well. Here are the first two paragraphs of an article. Note how concrete and specific details are used to create a mental picture of an Ethiopian restaurant that seems utterly real.

> The Ben Abeba restaurant is a spiral-shaped concrete confection perched on a mountain ridge near Lalibela, an Ethiopian town known for its labyrinth of the 12th-century churches hewn out of solid rock. The view is breathtaking: As the sun goes down, a spur of the Great Rift Valley stretches out seemingly miles below in subtly changing hues of green and brown, rolling away, fold after fold, as far as the eye can see. An immense lammergeyer, or bearded vulture, floats past, showing off its russet trousers.
>
> The staff, chivvied jovially along by an intrepid retired Scottish schoolmarm who created the restaurant a few years ago with an Ethiopian business partner, wrap yellow and white shawls around the guests against the sudden evening chill. The most popular dish is a spicy Ethiopian version of that old British staple, shepherd's pie, with minced goat's meat sometimes replacing lamb. Ben Abeba, whose name is a fusion of Scots and Amharic, Ethiopia's main language, is widely considered the best eatery in the highlands surrounding Lalibela, nearly 700 km (435 miles) north of Addis Ababa, the capital, by a bumpy road.

You probably won't need this level of concrete and specific details in your business writing. But in all your writing, you should remember that most people are more interested in the concrete, specific description that appeals to the senses than in abstract, intellectualized generalizations that appeal only to the mind.

2.2.4 Complete

Any writing or speaking that leaves readers wanting more information is not complete. Incomplete communication wastes everyone's time because he or she has to ask supplementary questions and the writer or speaker has to answer them. It just makes sense to put all the necessary information in your writing right from the start. For example:

➢ The finance committee will meet at 9 a.m.

Where is the committee meeting? Which date? The information is incomplete.

Better:

➢ The finance committee will meet in Room 202 at 9 a.m. on Tuesday, October 12.

The following is another example:

➢ The majority of Dell shareholders voted to merge with Apple Computer.

What kind of majority? If 90% of shareholders voted for the merger, that indicates strong support. If only 51% voted for the merger, then the shareholders are badly split on this move. The original sentence is incomplete—it doesn't give all the information that the CEO of Dell would want.

So, in all of your professional communication, whether written or spoken, aim to include all the necessary information. In other words, be complete.

2.2.5 Courteous

Writing courteously at work means following these guidelines:

Be Gender-neutral

Look at the following example:

➢ Each cabinet member must be responsible for the security of *his* briefcase.

Is the use of "his" correct? It's got the correct pronoun number, but many cabinet members these days are women, so using "his" is not gender-neutral. Today, military officers, police officers, lawyers, company officers, postal workers, doctors, nurses, firefighters, and even heavy-construction workers can be of either gender. So being gender-neutral which reflects your attitude is a kind of courtesy in professional writing.

Put the Reader First ("You" Rather than "We")

Putting the reader first is being tactful, which means considering other persons' feelings. "Courteous", in the business-communication sense, also means focusing all of your attention on the client or customer. For example:

➢ We have scheduled your appointment for September 2 at 3:00 p.m.

This sentence emphasizes "we". A more "you"-centered sentence is:

➢ Your appointment is scheduled for September 2 at 3:00 p.m.

Whenever possible, keep the "we" out of your professional communication and focus on "you"—the client, customer, or reader.

Of course, in some instances, you should avoid emphasizing "you". In a negative situation, such as when you mention bad news or correct a mistake, you typically should not use "you", to avoid placing blame. For example:

➢ You forgot to include your check with your order, so we can't send you the merchandise.

In this case, you should use the "we" form:

➢ We will be happy to send the merchandise when we receive your check.

2.2.6 Coherent

Coherent writing is writing that hangs together—the order of the words and the argument make logical sense, and each sentence and paragraph flows easily into the next. How can you make your writing coherent? Follow these guidelines:

Construct Paragraphs Carefully About One Topic

In all good writing, paragraphs develop one topic, and this topic is signaled by a topic sentence. The topic sentence, usually the first sentence, is the label stating what the paragraph is about.

In academic writing, paragraphs tend to be long—perhaps ten sentences or even more. There's a topic sentence with the main idea of the paragraph, but there can be many supporting subtopics and examples in an academic paragraph. In workplace writing, if you've got a paragraph like that—long, with lots of ideas and examples—then you should break that long paragraph down into two or more shorter paragraphs. The topic sentence for the first, shortened paragraph will serve as the topic sentence for the shorter, following paragraphs as well.

Write Sentences with One Main Idea

Sentences in business writing also present one idea within that topic—they don't veer off into tangled webs of related ideas as academic sentences sometimes do.

Although variety is important, within that variety, each sentence develops one main idea, not two or three. For business and professional writing, aim for several short sentences, with one idea per sentence with a variety of sentence structures, rather than long, complex, rambling sentences. For example:

> Jane Parker was planning to write about her recent trip to Beijing, where she saw many examples of Chinese paintings through the centuries, examples that, she felt, reflected the changing social conditions in China over time.

For business writing purposes, we should break the long sentence into two sentences, reflecting two ideas:

> Jane Parker was planning to write about her recent trip to Beijing, where she saw many examples of Chinese paintings through the centuries. These paintings, she felt, reflected the changing social conditions in China over time.

Use Transitional Words to Unite Sentences and Paragraphs

Transitional words are the glue that joins sentences and paragraphs into a pleasing, logical, and coherent unity.

Coherent writing needs transitions linking its sentences and paragraphs. Transitions can be classified into seven logical types: illustration, addition, contrast, similarity, causation, showing time, and showing space.

- Illustration transitions are words and phrases, such as "for example" "first of all" "such as", and so on. They show how X is an example of or similar to Y.
- Addition transitions are words and phrases, such as "also" "furthermore" "secondly" "in addition", and so on. They show how X and Y are linked or add something to each other.
- Contrast transitions are words and phrases, such as "although" "however" "on the contrary" "on the one hand...on the other hand", and so on. Contrast transitions

highlight how X is different from Y.

- Similarity transitions are words and phrases, such as "in the same way" "similarly" "just as", and so on. Similarity transitions highlight how X is similar to Y.
- Causation transitions are words and phrases, such as "because" "consequently" "as a result" "therefore", and so on. Causation transitions show that X caused Y or Y resulted from X.
- Transitions showing time include "after" "later" "while" "since then", and so on. Time transitions highlight how X and Y are related in time.
- Transitions showing space include "above" "in front of" "next to", and so on. Space transitions emphasize how X and Y are related in space.

For example:

> George spent six hours last night watching the Olympic Games. He was late for the morning meeting.

We can see the connection between these two sentences, but they are not coherent. How to fix it? Add a transition:

> George spent six hours last night watching the Olympic Games. *Therefore*, he was late for the morning meeting.

"Therefore" is a transitional word showing causation.

Be Consistent in Formatting Numbers

As part of coherence, numbers in business and professional writing need to be consistent when presented. The following outlines some widely accepted guidelines for presenting numbers in professional and business writing.

1) Spell out the numbers one to ten; use numerals for numbers 11 and above. For example:

    > We ordered *three* large dinners from Chinese takeout.

    > He has *13* books on loan from the library.

2) In technical documents, such as engineering, scientific, or economic reports, feel free to break the above rule. For example:

    > Keep PILOT LIGHT button down for *3* seconds and slowly release it.

3) Never start a sentence with a numeral. Either write the number out or rewrite the sentence to start with some other word. For example:

Chapter 2 Language Techniques for Effective Writing

> *2020* sales figures indicate a sharp decline in the fourth quarter.

It should be rewritten:

> Sales figures for *2020* indicate a sharp decline in the fourth quarter.

4) Spell out numbers that aren't precise figures. In addition, you would usually spell out numbers before terms, such as "dozen" "hundred" and "thousand". For example:

> He always has *a hundred* projects on the go.

> We ordered *four* dozen eggs.

5) Use figures for currency. Non-precise numbers in the millions and higher are usually expressed by a mixture of numerals and spelled-out numbers. For large numbers, million and trillion are usually spelled out. For example:

> The Whites spent *$48,000* renovating their house.

> Civil servants spent *$4* million on lattes last year.

> The government spent *$3.5* million on plastic figurines.

6) Use numerals for ages, years, dates, percentages, and addresses. For example:

> The *72*-year-old man retired after *48* years as a mechanic.

Begin Lists with the Same Grammatical Construction

All items in a list must begin with a noun, a verb, an adjective, a participle, or some other parts of speech to stick to coherence. Furthermore, parallelism in lists is a sign of elegant, carefully thought-out writing. Please remember: Lists that form a complete sentence end with a period or other appropriate punctuation. For example:

> Coherent writing

  I. has one idea per paragraph,

  II. has one idea per sentence,

  III. uses transitions to create a logical whole,

  IV. is consistent in its use of number, and

  V. begins lists with the same grammatical element.

2.2.7 Constructive

The seventh C is constructive. In professional writing, whenever possible, you want to put forward what you can do, not what you can't do. Similarly, you want to tell customers and clients what they can do, not what they can't do. It is, in other words, constructive.

Look at the following two signs:

Figure 2.1   Signs of prohibiting smoking

As for the above two signs, the sign on the right, which thanks customers, is more constructive than the one on the left, which issues an order.

Constructive writing also avoids words, such as "sorry" "regretfully" "unfortunately", and the like. These negative words all imply that you have either failed or cannot offer a service that customers might like, even if what you do offer is excellent.

Being constructive doesn't mean that you shouldn't apologize if you have genuinely made a mistake. When a company or individual genuinely makes a mistake, the best course of action—the most constructive course of action—is to admit the mistake, take responsibility, and vow to do better next time.

"Constructive" is also used in the sense of "constructive criticism", which means criticism that identifies problems and proposes solutions rather than blindly judging, blaming, or condemning.

The following table presents some examples of constructive expressions.

Table 2.9   Examples of constructive expressions

Instead of Using	Use
NO CHILDREN, NO PETS.	This building welcomes adults without pets.
Sorry, this bus is out of service.	All our operators are busy. We will be with you as soon as possible.
Sorry, but your package won't arrive until Wednesday.	Your package will be delivered on Wednesday.
You are a terrible writer.	If you used fewer passive verbs, your writing would be stronger.

Chapter 2 Language Techniques for Effective Writing

Just to repeat, here is the basic rule for constructive communication: say what you can do, not what you can't.

2.3 Active Voice Versus Passive Voice

In active voice sentences, the subjects usually do the action, as in "James [subject] prepared [action] the report [object]." Passive voice has the doer of the action as the object of the sentence: "The report [subject] was prepared [action] by James [object, but the doer of the action]." As discussed in the previous part, it is natural for an English sentence to use the active voice.

Active and passive voices in writing set the tone in every sentence. The active voice directly connects the action with the person who is performing that action. The passive voice renders the doer of the action less obvious if that person is ever identified at all. The active voice is concise and energetic, and it is the preferred writing style. For example:

➢ We recommend you file a claim. (active voice)

➢ It is recommended that you file a claim. (passive voice)

Passive voice has two characteristics: the use of a form of the auxiliary verb "be" and the implicit or explicit use of the preposition "by". If you stated "The report was prepared last week.", it is "implied" that the report was prepared "by" someone (not explicitly stated).

Why is the active voice preferable to the passive voice? One reason is that readers subconsciously pay more attention to action. Another reason is that sentences written in the active voice are shorter and more direct; therefore, they are easier to interpret.

In business writing, only 10% to 15% of your sentences should be structured in the passive voice. However, sometimes using the passive voice makes sense. Even though the active voice is more straightforward, there are times when passive voice is applied in formal documents or research studies.

When you may want to focus on the object rather than the subject:

➢ The sales report is published quarterly.

➢ Our proposal was submitted late because critical details were still missing.

When you want to emphasize the receiver:

> Hannah was accepted at Harvard Medical School.

> The data were analyzed to determine significant trends.

When you want to put some variation into your text, or smooth thought transition:

> This year's Mid-Autumn Festival Party will be held at Yuelu Park. It should be a warm and festive celebration—see you there!

Or you may also want to avoid assigning blame:

> The file was removed from the designated cabinet.

2.4　Positive and Unbiased Tones

Researchers have found that business people respond better to positive language than negative language, and they are also more likely to act on a positively worded request than one that uses negative words.

It is impossible to overstate the power of positive focus in your writing. Writing positively requires that your mind thinks in the same direction. So, focus on the good stuff, on what you can do, not on what you can't; and stay far away from negative thinking and a negative tone.

The tone you use in your writing plays a vital role in your ultimate success with any issue. It conveys your attitude, your personality, and even how you feel about your reader. In a business environment, you want to maintain the attention and goodwill of your reader. If you use a positive tone, you have a lower probability of alienating or offending your reader. Please compare the following two memos.

Here is a memo from a manager to his employees regarding an infraction in the dress code by one of his employees:

To: All Employees
From: Russ Yates
Date: October 1, 2021
Re: Dress Code

For women: Effective immediately, there will be no more short skirts allowed in the office.

Chapter 2 Language Techniques for Effective Writing

(Continued)

> This means anything above the mid-calf. Please review the dress code rules in your new hire packet. You may only wear skirts that are two inches above the knee. If you are caught wearing a short skirt, you will be sent home (unpaid) immediately.
>
> For men: Effective immediately, there will be no more jeans or sneakers allowed in the office. Please review the dress code rules in your new hire packet. Only wear dress slacks and shoes to work. A total disregard of these rules will mean that you will be sent home immediately and you will lose your pay for the day.

The above memo is condescending and challenging. It uses a negative term like "caught", which immediately puts people on the defensive. It not only puts off the employees who do abide by the dress code, but demonstrates the manager's clear lack of grace and warmth. Subordinates will not follow such an uncouth leader for long.

Here is how that manager can improve his writing style:

> **To:** All Employees
> **From:** Russ Yates
> **Date:** October 1, 2021
> **Re:** Dress Code
>
> Just a reminder about dress code regulations for men and women. Women: Please keep all skirts to two inches above the knee, no shorter. Men: Please refrain from wearing jeans and sneakers to the office. Take a quick minute to review company dress code policy—it is on pages 12–13 in your new hire packet. You may all dress comfortably for dress down Fridays. As always, my door remains open for any questions or concerns.
>
> Thanks for the continued great work—keep it up!

The revised memo reflects a positive and respectful tone. The readers—even the ones who broke the dress code rule—leave this letter with a much more positive feeling. They are reminded that the boss is paying attention to everything and is also there for them. There is no need to be threatening, as consequences for another infraction are already listed in the referenced new hire packet, and are imposed individually anyway.

You can establish a more positive tone in your writing at work by using the following techniques:

Avoid Negative Words or Words with a Negative Connotation

These are words like *impossible*, *terrible*, *never*, or *crisis*. Unless you are writing a letter that demands some negative content (like a collection letter), avoid negative words and phrases as much as possible.

Table 2.10 Words with a negative connotation

apologize	error	neglect
anxious	fail	never
avoid	fault	no
bad	hesitate	not
damage	impossible	problem
delay	inadequate	trouble
delinquent	incapable	unclear
deny	incomplete	unfortunate
difficulty	ineligible	unless
disapprove	lack	unreliable
dishonest	mistake	wrong

Don't Get Sloppy

Even though you should be warm and personal in your tone, be sure not to get sloppy with your writing. Remember that you are at work and that consistency with proper grammar and sentence structure is key to maintaining a positive professional image.

Cut Out "Angry" Words and Phrases

They do nothing more than provoke an argument, which is not your goal. Delete anything that sounds accusatory or patronizing: *lazy*, *alibi*, or *blame*. Avoid libelous words, such as *fraud*, *cheat*, or *unethical*, or you will need a lawyer before you know it. Remember that people with opinions differing from yours are not necessarily crazy or ignorant.

Show Enthusiasm

Let's face it: Eagerness and passion are contagious. People usually react well to a positive outlook. So, don't be afraid to use words or phrases like *beyond compare* or *invaluable asset* to emphasize the positive.

Chapter 2 Language Techniques for Effective Writing

Emphasize What You Can Do, Not What You Can't Do

Focus on the upside of the situation, and offer alternatives if possible.

Do More than You Have to—Go Above and Beyond

This means you should help someone even if you think it won't directly benefit you. Your tone has a way of opening—or closing—the most unexpected doors.

In addition to using a positive tone with your readers, you should also maintain an unbiased tone. That means you should use language that is free of bias regarding culture, gender, race and ethnicity, and age and disability.

Culture

Be aware of terminology that may not be understood by a reader from a culture where English is not the native language. Avoid slang, idioms, or acronyms in your messages to readers from other cultures.

Gender

Avoid words that wrongly exclude women or men. The following are some common expressions of gender bias, with unbiased alternatives.

Table 2.11   Examples of expressions of gender bias and unbiased alternatives

Instead of Using	Use
man-made	artificial/synthetic/manufactured
manpower	workers/personnel/workforce
businessman	business person
chairman	chairperson
waiter/waitress	server

Race and Ethnicity

Eliminate references that reinforce racial or ethnic stereotypes. It is best not to identify a person by race or ethnicity unless the identification is relevant to the material being discussed.

Age and Disability

Avoid references to a person's age or physical limitations unless it is relevant. Avoid using terms, such as *handicapped*, *crippled*, and *retarded*. If reference to a disability is a must,

39

refer to the person first and the disability second.

2.5 Punctuation

This section offers the rules for using punctuation correctly.

2.5.1 Commas

Commas are used in the following eight situations:

1) After an introductory word, phrase, or dependent clause. The introductory comma is used when the parts of a sentence are out of the "natural" order, that is, when part of the predicate goes before the subject or when a subordinate clause precedes an independent clause. For example:

    ➢ In the case of commas, it's best to follow the rules.

    ➢ Although lemon is tasty, I prefer sugar in my tea.

2) In academic and formal professional writing, before a coordinating conjunction, i.e. a conjunction that joins independent clauses. For example:

    ➢ This is a better question, but is still broad.

3) For a series or list of items. The serial (or "Oxford") comma—a comma before the final conjunction "and"—is required in academic writing. However, a comma is, in non-academic writing, optional after the second-last item in the series. The rule: Decide whether you'll use the serial comma or not in a piece of writing and then be consistent. For example:

    ➢ In general, the research background, literature review, research objectives, methodology, and timetable have been provided in this proposal.

    ➢ George ate Spam, toast, eggs and asparagus for breakfast.

4) To introduce a dialog or a quotation in dialog form. For example:

    ➢ He said, "I want my rights respected!"

5) To set off non-essential or "interrupting" words, phrases, or clauses. These are words, phrases, or clauses that, if removed, would not change the meaning of a sentence. For

Chapter 2 Language Techniques for Effective Writing

example:

➢ A copy of our analysis, along with our interpretation of its results, is enclosed.

6) When you are talking about the same noun twice but using different words. In grammar, this renaming of a noun is called an appositive, so the surrounding commas are called appositive commas. For example:

➢ Extrasensory perception (ESP), the sixth sense, is the ability to perceive information without using the five physical senses.

7) When an element at the end of the sentence offers a shift in the idea of what's gone before or is an aside not essential to the meaning of the main clause. For example:

➢ Many fail to consider the importance of grammar to writing, if they think about grammar at all.

8) To separate dates, addresses, or geographical names. For example:

➢ He lived at 999 Stanmer Park Road, Brighton, UK, from February 1, 2016 to January 31, 2017.

2.5.2 Periods

Periods are used in the following situations:

1) Use periods at the end of sentences that neither exclaim nor ask a question, but simply make a statement. For example:

➢ I think the company newspaper should come out only twice a month.

2) Use periods to follow some abbreviations and contractions. For example:

➢ Dr. Martin Luther King Jr. was born on January 15, 1929, in Atlanta, Georgia.

3) Use periods with an individual's initials. For example:

➢ F. Scott Fitzgerald's *Tales of the Jazz Age* (1922) was a classic representation of the period.

4) Use periods after numbers and letters in listings and outlines. For example:

➢ Please have the following on my desk by Monday:

   a. two copies of your department needs assessment;

   b. your budget outline;

   c. your goals and objectives for the quarter.

2.5.3 Question Marks

The question mark is the easiest mark to use. Here are three good rules for using it.

1) Use a question mark when you're seeking information. Often, people in business are seeking information from each other. In talking, they'd simply say something like this:

    ➢ How many people in your department will be taking annual leave in June?

2) Use a question mark as a tag at the end of a sentence. For example:

    ➢ Autumn is the golden season of Changsha City, isn't it?

You're not seeking information and surely don't expect an answer. You just want more emphasis than the period would give.

3) Ask a question you're going to answer. For example:

    ➢ Why is June a good time for people in our company to take annual leave? The main reason is that our workload will be lower then but will pick up its normal pace in July and August.

The question draws your readers in and gets them to pay attention to the answer. One good use of this type of question is to hook your reader at the beginning of a report or article.

2.5.4 Semicolons

The main function of a semicolon is to separate similar grammatical units. Think of it as the point of balance between two ideas. Knowing when a semicolon is needed is easy—there are only two basic uses.

1) Use a semicolon to join independent clauses. This is the most common use of a semicolon. For example:

    ➢ June is a good time for a vacation; February usually isn't.

    ➢ Practice doesn't make perfect; practice makes permanent.

Notice there's a full sentence on each side of the semicolon. Sometimes there's a word or a phrase that explicitly says what the relationship is between the two sentences—words or phrases like *however*, *for example*, and *therefore*. For example:

    ➢ Practice doesn't make perfect; however, practice makes permanent.

2) Use a semicolon to separate certain complicated phrases. For example:

    ➢ We ate crab cakes, simmered in sauce; steak, rare to the point of being blood-red; potatoes, sliced and baked with cumin powder; and asparagus, crunchy and smothered in butter.

2.5.5 Colons

Colons have only four uses.

1) To introduce some sort of list or elucidation. These colons say "Get ready because here is my explanation or catalog of items." For example:

   ➢ Location, location, location: This is the mantra of the real estate agent.

2) To introduce a quotation. For example:

   ➢ Edgar was emphatic: "I demand my rights!"

Both colons and commas can be used correctly to introduce quotations. The colon before a quotation is more common when what is being quoted is lengthy, as in academic writing.

3) Following the greeting in a business letter. For example:

   ➢ Dear Ms. McInerny:

4) Between a title and a subtitle. For example:

   ➢ The Art of Archery: A Master's Guide

2.5.6 Dashes

The dash is a terrific mark of punctuation, often replacing a comma and adding emphasis. Here are two good uses for it.

1) Use a dash at the end of a sentence to emphasize what comes next. For example, you can have a dash followed by a word, a list, or even another sentence:

   ➢ There's one month that's better than any other for a vacation—June.

   ➢ These are the best months for a vacation—June, July, and August.

   ➢ June is a great month for a vacation—the weather is perfect.

2) Use dashes to emphasize an idea in the middle of a sentence. For example:

   ➢ The reviewers looked at everything in the files—including last month's payroll records—and found everything correct.

Compare:

   ➢ The reviewers looked at everything in the files—including last month's payroll records—and found everything correct.

> The reviewers looked at everything in the files, including last month's payroll records, and found everything correct.

> The reviewers looked at everything in the files (including last month's payroll records) and found everything correct.

The difference is the amount of emphasis:

- Dashes emphasize the most.
- Commas are standard.
- Parentheses are like a whispered aside.

There are three kinds of dashes:

1) the em dash (—);
2) the en dash (–);
3) the half en dash (-).

Here are their uses:

- Use the em dash for most punctuation.
- Use the en dash to mean "to" (e.g. 2–4 p.m.).
- Use the half en dash for hyphenated words and breaks in words at the ends of lines. Another name for the half en dash is the hyphen.

Newspapers sometimes use the en dash instead of the em dash. That's because the en dash is a space saver for the narrow columns of text.

Hyphenated compounds are always joined using a hyphen (e.g. the verb "cross-examine"). We are concerned here with a special type of compound word—in grammar, the compound modifier, meaning two or more adjectives or modifying words joined together with hyphens. Hyphens between these modifiers increase clarity. For example:

> Sheila asked the salesperson for a *little-used* car.

When we form a compound between some adverbs not ending with "ly" and a second modifier, it is suitable to use a hyphen:

> It was a *much-needed* policy.

> That is the *worst-paid* job.

2.5.7 Quotation Marks

Quotation marks have four uses.

1) Quotation marks are used to identify quotations or parts of quotations, and sometimes to give special emphasis to certain words or phrases. Most of the time, quotation marks follow the punctuation. For example:

   ➢ "I'm going into town," said Mark. "Can I buy you anything?"

2) Quotation marks can also be used in a sentence to highlight a word or phrase for emphasis when you intend a word or phrase to be read as ironic and want to distance yourself from it (sometimes called "scare quotes"), or when you are using slang. For example:

   ➢ Ben told us he was "tired", but a better word is "lazy".

3) Periods, commas, semicolons, colons, question marks, exclamation marks, and dashes go outside closing quotation marks unless the punctuation is part of the quoted material. For example:

   ➢ According to Bill Gates, "Intellectual property has the shelf life of a banana"; it's a good thing he didn't substitute the word "apple".

   ➢ She asked, "What's the worst that could happen if we put all our eggs into one basket?"

   ➢ Who said, "Never put all your eggs in one basket"?

4) If you are putting a quotation inside another quotation, then use double quotation marks for the outside quotation and single quotation marks for the inside quotation. For example:

   ➢ Harriet said, "Ben told us he was 'tired', but a better word is 'lazy'."

Double quotation marks are the default style for writing in North America. However, single quotation marks are often used in formal British English. For a quotation within a quotation, the traditional British style is the mirror image of the North American style: internal quotations take double quotation marks.

American newspapers, magazines, and newsletters tend to use single quotation marks for quoted material in headlines, headings, and (sometimes) captions.

2.5.8　Parentheses and Brackets

Parentheses are round, like this: ( ). Brackets are square, like this: [ ], although parentheses are often referred to as brackets. Parentheses and brackets are used to enclose additional and usually non-essential information ("parenthetical information", in grammar). Here are a few common uses.

1) Parentheses are used to present acronyms or abbreviations. For example:

   ➢ The World Health Organization (WHO) reported new cases of Ebola virus disease this July.

2) Parentheses are used to enclose numerals that confirm spelled out numbers or that distinguish items in a list. For example:

   ➢ This contract expires in forty-eight (48) hours.

   ➢ The important steps in choosing a good password are: (1) use at least six characters; (2) mix numbers and letters and punctuation marks; (3) use both upper and lower case; and (4) be random in your choice.

3) Brackets are used to identify an editorial insertion into a quotation. The bracketed material sometimes inserts information provided elsewhere in the original text. For example:

   ➢ He [the airline pilot] claimed he saw an unidentified flying object (UFO) during his landing at Springfield Airport.

4) Brackets are also used to enclose parenthetical content within a parenthetical element. In other words, if you need parentheses within parentheses, you choose brackets. For example:

   ➢ The airline pilot claimed he saw a UFO during his landing at Springfield airport. (Perhaps he'd just watched the recent rerun of *Close Encounters of the Third Kind* [1977] on television.)

5) If an entire sentence is within parentheses, then the closing punctuation is also within the parentheses. If the parentheses enclose only part of a sentence, the punctuation goes outside the parentheses. For example:

   ➢ Semicolons can be used to join independent clauses (sometimes with a conjunctive adverb).

Chapter 2 Language Techniques for Effective Writing

2.5.9 Ellipses

What is the function of an ellipsis? It's a wonderful mark. The ellipsis should be part of your arsenal.

1) Use an ellipsis to show a reflective or dramatic pause. Think of the ellipsis as a dash with something extra. It adds emphasis by pausing for a beat or two. For example:

   ➢ Minnesota is beautiful in summer...wonderland of lakes and forests.

2) Use an ellipsis to show that a list could be much longer. The ellipsis also serves as a pause in this usage, a pause for the reader to understand that the list could go on and on. For example:

   ➢ My favorite sports are basketball and volleyball and football and...I'm crazy about ball games!

3) Use an ellipsis to show you've left out words in a quotation. When you're quoting someone else, you don't always need to include every word. To show your reader you've left out something, just replace the missing words with an ellipsis. For example:

   ➢ One of the fascinating things about Charles Darwin is that he really does seem to have been one of those men whose careers quite unexpectedly and fortuitously are decided for them by a single stroke of fortune. For twenty-two years nothing much happens, no exceptional abilities are revealed; then suddenly a chance is offered...and away he soars into the blue never to return.

You wouldn't change the meaning by leaving out those words, but you need to show your reader that you're not giving a complete quote. By the way, you don't need to use an ellipsis to show you've left out words from the beginning or end of a quotation, just the middle. The ellipsis just adds clutter in these cases and doesn't give substantial help to your reader.

❯ Exercises

1. **The sentences below contain errors in terms of the seven Cs. Find the errors and correct them. Give your explanation.**

   1) The entrance exam was failed by one-third of the applicants.

   2) Children under 12 years old cannot participate in the competition.

3) We are pleased to inform you that we have selected you for an interview for the executive secretary position.

4) He distributed annual reports to the recipients bound in white and blue covers.

5) A new photocopier is needed by the employees in the Foreign Affairs Division.

2. *Several types of transitions are used in the following paragraph about a company's poor sales, which is reprinted below. Identify them for the bolded words or phrases in the example.*

    In the past month, our company's sales have gone down 30%. **As a result**, our cash flow situation has become critical. **Worse**, this loss of revenue could even threaten our company's future. **Therefore**, we need to take action to prevent bankruptcy, **including** working harder to get sales and cutting our production costs.

3. *Decide whether the following sentences are vague or clear.*

1) Your investment should increase significantly by next year.

2) Your investment should increase 20% by next year.

3) The new system has been very profitable.

4) The new system has reduced operating costs by 30%.

5) The project is somewhat behind schedule.

6) The project is one week late.

Chapter 3
Document Design

Reading can become tedious if good design is not factored into what your eyes must look at. One of the most important elements of writing in the workplace is the document's appearance. Writing in professional contexts requires as much attention to the way a document appears on the page or the screen as its content. The reason is that as writers, we must make the task of reading easy for our readers.

In this chapter, we'll cover the basics of document design for the print and screen. We will discuss the conventions of document design as they pertain to specific genres. This chapter provides you with formatting techniques to use. These techniques will help you to improve the readability of your documents and increase the readers' understanding of the content.

In this chapter, you will learn about:

- the importance of good document design;
- choosing typefaces carefully;
- using "chunking" to communicate;
- creating good headings;
- using a good layout for columns and lists;
- using block paragraphing and white space effectively;
- incorporating visuals.

3.1 The Importance of Good Document Design

As with your writing, the documents that present your writing to the world, whether in print or on the computer, are a reflection of you and your professionalism.

"Layout" means the overall look of your page—from the typeface you choose to how much space you put above and below your headings. Making good choices can make all the difference.

Here are some of the advantages of a good layout:

- If your document looks good, people will more likely pick it up.
- A good layout makes your document look professional. The right typefaces, the right

spacing, and all the other small choices working together add up to a professional image.

- A good layout helps readers to see the parts of a document—and know where they are in it.

Those are all advantages to have a good layout, but there's a more important advantage: When you learn the value of headings and lists, you begin to use them. That means you bring structure to your writing and it becomes better-organized.

So a good layout doesn't just mean showing your reader the parts of your document; it also means creating a document with parts in the first place. A good layout, then, helps your page look good and more.

Some people wonder if they should use headings and indented lists in letters, memos, emails, and web pages. Of course! Headings and indented lists don't care if they are in letters or not—and neither do most readers. Readers don't think about formats. ("Oh, this is an email. It shouldn't have headings!") Readers just read for content, trying to find out what the writer is saying. So if headings serve to label parts of a report, they can also label parts of a letter, a memo, an email, or a web page. The same value to the reader is there.

3.2 Choosing Typefaces Carefully

Before you put a word on a page, you should decide what typefaces you want to use. Fonts are styles of typefaces.

3.2.1 Serifs Versus Sans Serif

What does the term "serif" mean? A "serif" is the little icicle that hangs from the ends of letter crossbars and at the feet of letter uprights. Serif fonts are commonly used for the text of textbooks, newspapers, and magazines. "Sans serif" fonts ("sans" in French means "without"), on the other hand, don't have the icicles and are relatively smooth fonts. Sans serif fonts are typically used in print documents for headings and the text in tables and charts. Here's an illustration of both fonts:

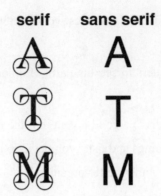

Figure 3.1 An illustration of the serif font and sans serif font

The typeface on the left is Times New Roman. It has serifs. The typeface on the right, without serifs, is Arial.

Each type of font has advantages and disadvantages. The serif fonts, such as Times New Roman, are easier to read in long sentences and paragraphs of text than sans serif fonts: The serifs "guide" the eye from one letter to the next. Also, serif font letters vary in width, so they "fit" together, which also offers an easy pathway for the eye by compressing type.

On the other hand, the letters of sans serif fonts are a bit wider than serif fonts and they don't "fit" together as serif fonts do. As a result, sans serif fonts are "sticky" on the eyes; each letter and word stands out more than it would in a serif font. As sans serif fonts attract the eye and are different from a serif font, which is often selected for the body of a document, they are excellent for headings and easily act as signposts for the reader of your document. In short, sans serif headings are, again, reader-friendly.

3.2.2 Choosing a Typeface with Serifs for Body Text

Most publications in the United States—well over 95%—use a typeface with serifs for the body text. Body text means, essentially, all of the paragraphs but not the titles, headings, illustrations, and so forth.

Times New Roman is by far the most common typeface for body text in business writing—and it's a great choice. If you use Times New Roman for your body text, the standard size is 12 point. That's a good size most of the time. (By the way, Georgia is a common font with serifs for web pages. It was designed with web pages in mind.)

3.2.3 Using a Sans Serif Typeface for Headings and Illustrations

The standard for years has been to use a typeface with serifs for body text but a sans serif typeface for most headings. Here, "standard" doesn't mean the right way or the only way—just the most common way.

If you look at publications in a bookstore, you'll find that the sans serif typeface is used in most headings. Sans serif works well as a heading because:

- sans serif is clearly different from serifs (the usual body text typefaces);
- sans serif has a clean, uncluttered look in boldface (and you want to make most of your headings bold).

Sans serif is also a good choice for your text for tables, illustrations, indented quotations, sidebars, and so forth. That's because these items normally need a smaller size (usually 2 points smaller than the body text). A typeface with serifs in a small size can look cluttered and busy; a sans serif typeface doesn't.

There are some choices for your reference: Most people in business use 12-point Times New Roman for all of their body text; they use Arial for headings (there's no standard size because headings can vary so much), labels (such as for graphs) and illustrations (such as for the text in a table or a flow chart), and the most common type size for these is 10 point.

3.2.4 Italic Versus Bold

When you want to emphasize a word or a phrase within a paragraph, use italic instead of bold. Bold stands out too much, from several feet away. Reserve bold for headings and titles. Italic type, on the other hand, stands out as you read it—perfect for words and phrases within paragraphs.

3.2.5 Other Tips

It is more standard to make the headings in boldface, as well as to use upper case and lower case letters, instead of all capital letters. Upper case and lower case letters keep the eye moving and increase the reading speed by 19%.

Table 3.1 Use of upper case and lower case letters in headings

Instead of Using	Use
FORMATTING TECHNIQUES FOR EFFECTIVE WRITING	Formatting Techniques for Effective Writing
A STEP-BY-STEP APPROACH TO BUSINESS AND PROFESSIONAL WRITING	A Step-by-step Approach to Business and Professional Writing

3.3 Using "Chunking" to Communicate

In some cases, such as business letters, the layout is fixed: you will always use "full-block" formatting for letters and the body of memos, for example. But what about documents, such as brochures, flyers, reports, web pages, and the like? What kind of overall design strategy should you follow for more complex kinds of layouts? The answer, in one word, is "modular". Modules are short "chunks" of text or graphics that the reader can take in with a glance before going on to the next "chunk". In other words, rather than giving the reader a long, gray column or page of text, a modular layout breaks the text and pictures into smaller bits that the reader can, as it were, easily "swallow" without a lot of reading or viewing effort.

Readers absorb information more rapidly if it is presented to them in easy-to-process sections or "chunks". Short sections break up the material into easily understood segments. This is the approach you want to take in designing documents. You give the reader a bite-size chunk of information just like one potato chip, as it were. It can be an arresting headline, a short paragraph of fascinating text, an intriguing photograph or a graphic. Then you lead the reader's eye to another bite-size chunk of information, and another, until the reader has, almost without any conscious effort, read the whole document.

Readers now want a less demanding look at their news and other documents. The preferred design style today follows more of a "potato-chip" approach—a modular approach. For example:

Figure 3.2　A modular layout for a web page

Figure 3.2 shows a model for feature web pages. And Figure 3.3 is a screenshot of the UC Berkeley graduate application web page. Note, again, the short "chunks" of information, the boxes, the lists, and the color, all aim to make this page very easy to read.

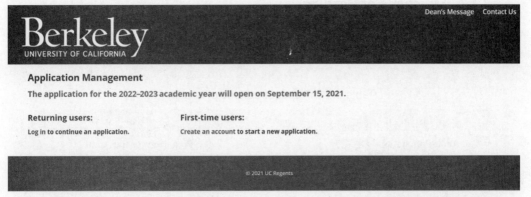

Figure 3.3   A modular layout for the UC Berkeley Graduate Application web page

The easiest way to "chunk" material in your document is to use headings. A rule of thumb to consider is that if you have four or five paragraphs of straight text, determine if a heading is useful to "chunk" the information. In addition to breaking the material into sections, headings attract your readers' attention to important information. Headings also help your readers to find their ways through a document and locate contents they are interested in.

3.4   Creating Good Headings

Whenever you write anything longer than a page, you'll probably want to use headings (and they work fine in documents less than a page, too). You already know to choose a sans serif typeface for most headings. This section will give you other tips so your headings will be efficient and attractive.

3.4.1   Reasons to Use Headings

You'll want to use headings in anything longer than a page because they:

- show your readers at a glance that your document is organized;
- label the parts of your document;
- show where parts begin and end (replacing the need for strong verbal transitions);

- help your readers to find the parts of your document they need to read;
- help you to organize your writing in the first place.

3.4.2　Structures of Headings

Make the headings grammatically parallel and reduce wordiness. An example is set in the following table.

Table 3.2　Proper structures of headings

Instead of Using	Use
Audit Preparation	Preparing for the Audit
Conduct the Audit	Conducting the Audit
How to Respond to Findings	Responding to Findings

The original three headings are not parallel grammatically in structure, including a noun structure, a verb phrase and a "how-to" structure. After revision, we get three new gerund structures, which make the headings look neat and consistent.

3.4.3　Using at Least Two Headings of Each Type

Headings label the parts of your document. It's a label for one of several parts. If you have only one part, skip the heading and (for a report) use a title. For a memo or email, rely on the subject line. A letter, which has neither a title nor a subject line, relies on a strong beginning. So using at least two headings of each type is a basic principle.

3.4.4　Informative Headings Versus Engaging Headings

Sometimes simple headings, such as "Technical Analysis" and "Fundamental Analysis" are clear enough. Too often, though, writers use overly brief headings when something longer would be better. For example, instead of saying "Results", consider saying "Our Sales Are Improving". That way, readers who are skimming still get the most important information just by reading your headings.

You might also want to consider headings that engage your readers. For example, instead of saying "Our Sales Are Improving", you could make your heading a question: "How Are Our Sales This Quarter?" Questions usually draw your readers into the content of your section. Therefore, it's possible to have good headings that don't carry much information at all about the subject matter but are still effective because they pique the reader's interest. In other words, they are uninformative but engaging headings.

Informative headings are preferable whenever readers are trying to get information as quickly as possible. Engaging headings are suitable for more optional reading—marketing material, for instance.

3.4.5 More Space Above than Below Your Headings

One of the most common design mistakes with headings is putting the same space above and below them. The headings seem connected with the parts below them, the parts they label, don't they? They are clearly part of what they label, becoming a unit with the text below. So always put more space above than below your headings.

3.4.6 Down-style Headings

Lots of people today still use initial capital letters for each important word: "Our Sales Are Improving". People call that an "up-style" heading. Many professionals at work today prefer the down-style: "Our sales are improving". Boldface and a larger type size then set the headings apart from the body text. For example:

Many experts believe the answer is "probably not". To see why, let's look at two prominent types of stock forecasting:

- Technical analysis
- Fundamental analysis

Technical analysis

Technical analysis means looking at stock charts. Suppose a stock has gone up every day for the past 30 days. Can we assume it *will* go up again tomorrow? The answer is "no". Well, can we assume it's *likely* to go up tomorrow? The answer is "probably not".

Or suppose that every time Techronics has dropped from 45 to 30, it has bottomed out and begun climbing again. Can we assume that when it drops to 30 again, it will rise? No.

Lots of research shows that past performance is not a reliable indicator of future performance. According to Burton Malkiel in *A Random Walk Down Wall Street*, "The stock market has little, if any, memory."

In the above part of a memo, the heading, "Technical analysis", illustrates what a down-style heading is.

3.4.7 Differentiating Levels of Headings

If you need more than one level of headings, you can use different levels of headings, but you'd want to be certain that a reader clearly understands that your subheadings are subordinate to your headings. That is, you'd want your subheadings to look very different from your headings. For example, you wouldn't want your headings to be left-justified, bold, 14-point type and your subheadings to be just the same except 12-point type. Readers may not notice the subtle difference. Instead, make sure your subheadings are subordinate in at least two ways. For example, consider these possible designs in Table 3.3 for two levels of headings.

Table 3.3 Ways of differentiating a heading from a subheading

Possible Heading Style	Possible Subheading Style
Centered	Left-justified
14-point Arial	12-point Arial
Bold	Bold

With this design, your readers should have no trouble telling a heading from a subheading.

3.5 Using a Good Layout for Columns and Lists

You can vary column widths and use more than one column to make your document more attractive. Create columns when you want to compare information, define terms, provide troubleshooting tips, or summarize the material. You can combine the application of lists with columns. Create bulleted or numbered lists to emphasize a series of items in a visually clear way.

3.5.1 A Layout for Columns

Most documents on letter-size 8½-by-11-inch paper look fine with one column, left-justified. Left-justified means the text on the right margin is not straight; this is also called ragged right. Fully-justified text has both left and right margins straight; being fully-justified is how the text in most books is printed. You can divide the text into more than one column. But with two or more columns, you will want to make your text size smaller because columns are designed to make smaller text readable.

Here's an example of a narrow column in a 12-point font, with full-justification. The words seem oddly spaced and not that attractive. Sentences seem choppy and are not easy to read.

> Another option is to divide the text into more than one column, fully-justified. A warning, though: if you do so, you will want to make your text size smaller because narrow columns were designed to make smaller text readable.

Figure 3.4   A narrow column in a 12-point font with full-justification

Here's what the column looks like in a smaller font size, 10 point:

> Another option is to divide the text into more than one column, fully-justified. A warning, though: if you do so, you will want to make your text size smaller because narrow columns were designed to make smaller text readable.

Figure 3.5   A narrow column in a 10-point font with full-justification

Anyhow, you should adopt whichever column strategy that gives you the most attractive and readable page.

3.5.2   Application of Lists

Whenever you want to show more than one aspect of something, consider using an indented (or "bulleted") list. For instance, consider using an indented list if you have two or more of these: reasons, methods, examples, steps, conclusions, recommendations, etc.

And the marks in front of the items (•) are "bullets" which are commonplace in business writing because they instantly let readers see that there's more than one aspect of something.

Bullets or Numbers

If the order of the items in the list is important, such as when you are explaining steps in a process, use a numbered list. A numbered list implies sequence. For example:

➢ To assemble this desk, do the following:
  1. Unpack the numbered wooden panels.
  2. Lay out the screws and bolts.
  3. Attach wooden panel A to wooden panel B using the #4 screws.
  4. Attach wooden panel C to panel D using the #4 bolted screws...

Here is another example:

➢ There are three stages of work-related writing:
  1. assessing,
  2. writing, and
  3. evaluating.

If the order of the items is not important, such as in a list of options, use a bulleted list. For example:

➢ This Ikea desk package contains the following:
  - 12 #4 screws,
  - 12 #4 bolted screws,
  - 1 Phillips screwdriver, and
  - everything else necessary to build your desk.

When you create a bulleted or numbered list, introduce the list with a lead-in sentence so the reader knows about what he or she is going to read. Add more discussion after the list, if needed.

Parallelism

Whenever you make a list, you want to be sure that it's grammatically parallel. That is, you should try to put the items in parallel grammatical form. Creating a parallel list builds a rhythm into the material, which the reader subconsciously picks up, and it makes the material easier to interpret.

To make all items in a list parallel in grammatical structure, all list items must begin with the same grammatical element: a noun, a verb, an adjective, a participle, or whatever you choose. In the example above, the Ikea desk package example shows that each item in the contents list begins with a noun; in the numbered list each item usually begins with a verb that introduces a complete imperative sentence.

Good Spacing for Your Bulleted Lists

Just let your word processor automatically handle the spacing for your bullets. The defaults are probably just fine. However, if you look around at professional publications, you'll see many good variations. Newspapers, for example, usually don't indent the bullets at all from the left. That's fine because, with several columns of text on the page, too much indenting would make the page look fragmented.

Punctuating Your Bulleted Lists

There is no single system for punctuating bulleted lists. There aren't even any standards for punctuating your bulleted lists. Different companies have different rules. But any system is fine. Just be consistent. Some start with the traditional system which simply keeps all the punctuation and the word "and". For example:

> ➤ Our company is about to buy new equipment: computers, printers, and fax machines. (original)
>
> ➤ Our company is about to buy new equipment:
>   - computers,
>   - printers, and
>   - fax machines.

That system is fine. Sometimes we can use a slightly different one. If the items in the indented list are not full sentences, get rid of the commas and often the word "and". But we suggest a period at the end of the list. For example:

> ➤ Our company is about to buy
>   - computers
>   - printers
>   - fax machines.

And if the bulleted items are all sentences, then make them look like sentences. For example:

➤ Our company is about to buy new equipment:
- We're ordering five new computers.
- We're ordering two color printers.
- We're ordering three fax machines.

In addition, semicolons are also often used at the end of list items. It might be appropriate (and necessary for easy reading) to use them if the list items are long and have internal punctuation. Here's an example of a list with internal punctuation:

➤ When you use crayons,
- be sure to use vivid colors, which will attract the most attention;
- don't press too hard on the crayon, which might break it;
- don't cross the lines when you are coloring.

Bulleted Paragraphs

You don't have to limit bullets to words, phrases, or even single sentences. Full paragraphs are fine. By using bulleted paragraphs, you show that those paragraphs are related.

For example, suppose you've studied the need for a new parking lot. You've led a task force that concludes your company needs a new lot and has two reasons for that conclusion. Bulleted paragraphs can effectively lay out those conclusions:

➤ After meeting with contractors, the task force has decided to recommend we build a new parking lot for these two reasons:
- We expect to hire 200 new people in the next year. Because our parking lot is full now, with people looking for space every morning, there will be no good place for new employees to park unless we build a new lot. No other lots are available within a five-block radius.
- This is a favorable time to finance a new parking lot. Interest rates are at the lowest point in several years. Rates may rise in the future. We can afford a loan now, but if we wait, we may not be able to finance the parking lot.

There's a refinement you can use with bulleted paragraphs—add headings:

> After meeting with contractors, the task force has decided to recommend we build a new parking lot for these two reasons:

- *New hires.* We expect to hire 200 new people in the next year. Because our parking lot is full now, with people looking for space every morning, there will be no good place for new employees to park unless we build a new lot. No other lots are available within a five-block radius.

- *Low interest rates.* This is a favorable time to finance a new parking lot. Interest rates are at the lowest point in several years. Rates may do anything in the future. We can afford a loan now, but if we wait, we may not be able to.

Please note that don't use boldface for these headings because they'll stand out too much, drawing your reader's eyes to a relatively subordinate part of your page. Instead, use italic type. The technique of bulleted paragraphs is a great one to learn—and useful time after time.

3.6 Using Block Paragraphing and White Space Effectively

Block paragraphing means:

- non indenting the first line of your paragraphs;
- putting space between all paragraphs.

In the past, the preference was to indent the first lines of paragraphs. Now, the layout has changed. More and more business documents use headings, lists, and illustrations of all sorts. So much is happening on the left margin that indenting first lines can add confusion—making the page look disorganized.

You may wonder if you should justify your paragraphs. That is, should both the right and left margins be squared off? Or should you use a ragged right margin? Either way is fine; it's your choice. Virtually all typefaces today are proportional and do a reasonably good job with full justification.

White space is simply the open, empty space on the document page. It makes your document easier to read because it attracts the reader's attention and helps the reader to organize the information being presented.

To develop effective white space, you should observe some simple techniques. Provide margins of at least 1 inch on the top, bottom, left, and right sides of the page. If you are binding your document, provide at least a 2-inch margin on the left side of the page to allow for the binding. The right margin can be a ragged right margin (left justification) or an aligned right margin (full justification). A ragged right margin provides a more informal feeling than an aligned right margin.

Please bear the following in your mind:

- Place at least one blank line above and below each heading to supply white space around the heading.
- Double space between items in a list when the items are two or more lines long.
- Place a blank line between paragraphs that are single-spaced.
- Provide vertical spacing between columns.

The following is a sample memo with a good layout:

body text: 12-point Times New Roman

To: Mackenzie Melton
From: Sophia Hiller
Date: May 26, 2021
Subject: Is accurate stock forecasting possible?

italic (not underlining)

You asked me to look into the subject of *stock forecasting* and let you know what I found out. The issue is whether investors can forecast whether a particular stock is likely to go up or down. For example, is it possible to predict whether Techronics stock is likely to go up during the next month? Or year? Or five years?

Many experts believe the answer is "probably not". To see why, let's look at two prominent types of stock forecasting:

bullets

- Technical analysis

Chapter 3   Document Design

(Continued)

- Fundamental analysis

Technical analysis

one space after all punctuation

Technical analysis means looking at stock charts. Suppose a stock has gone up every day for the past 30 days. Can we assume it *will* go up again tomorrow? The answer is "no". Well, can we assume it's *likely* to go up tomorrow? The answer is "probably not".

Or suppose that every time Techronics has dropped from 45 to 30, it has bottomed out and begun climbing again. Can we assume that when it drops to 30 again, it will rise? No.

Lots of research shows that past performance is not a reliable indicator of future performance. According to Burton Malkiel in *A Random Walk Down Wall Street*, "The stock market has little, if any, memory."

Fundamental analysis

em dash (not two hyphens)

Fundamental analysis means looking at a company's value—and trying to determine its future earnings. To do that, analysts consider the management of a company, the future demand for its product, the possible risks involved, the dividends it's paying, etc.

For example, suppose an analyst spends time at Techronics and believes the company has a great product, great financing, a great management team, and tremendous growth potential. He also believes the market has undervalued the Techronics stock. Does that mean the stock is likely to go up? Some experts would say, "Buy!" Others would say, "Hmmmm...I think I'll just put my money in index funds."

In other words, experts are more inclined to accept fundamental analysis than technical analysis; however, there's still lots of controversy and disagreement about its practical effectiveness.

headings: 12-point bold Arial, down style

block paragraphs

more space above heading than below

3.7 Incorporating Visuals

Visuals capture the attention of your reader. Incorporating visuals in your documents helps you to convey information more easily to your reader. It is estimated that people obtain as much as 80% of learning through the eye. Visuals can depict key relationships, such as comparisons, trends, and parts of a whole. They can summarize and condense information in a relatively small space. Visuals can be very persuasive when you are trying to get others to accept your position.

Selecting appropriate visuals for your intended reader is very important. Consider how the reader will use the visuals. Determine why the reader needs the visuals. Consider the technical ability of your reader to interpret visuals. If you want to compare sales of three products for salespersons, a bar graph might be appropriate. If you want to show quarterly trends of the product sales for sales executives, a multiple-line graph would be an appropriate choice. The following table illustrates different purposes or uses for different types of visuals.

Table 3.4 Visual types and purposes

Types	Purposes
Table	Organize numerical data or information into rows and columns.
Bar or column chart	Show data in vertical or horizontal columns for comparison.
Gantt chart	Plan and track status of the project with beginning and end dates.
Line chart	Illustrate trends over time; compare data over time.
Map	Show specific points within an area; illustrate distances; show geographic features.
Organizational chart	Depict hierarchies within an organization; show how elements relate to one another.
Photograph	Illustrate actual images; record events.
Pie chart	Show parts of a whole adding up to 100%.

3.7.1 Tables, Charts, and Graphs

Tables, charts, and graphs are a great way of presenting a lot of information in a format that is easier to read than a paragraph of text. In most tables, words and numbers are set in columns for easy reference. Suppose you are presenting the sales figures for four of the regions in your company. You can write the following:

> In 2020, Hunan had sales of RMB 2,300,000, Hubei RMB 2,832,000, and Fujian RMB 2,050,000, while sales in Jiangxi were RMB 1,725,000.

Or, for better readability, you can put these figures into a table, as follows:

Table 3.5   Regional sales figures for 2020

Regions	Sales
Hunan	RMB 2,300,000
Hubei	RMB 2,832,000
Fujian	RMB 2,050,000
Jiangxi	RMB 1,725,000
Total	RMB 8,907,000

With a table, the reader can see the regional and total sales at a glance, which doesn't happen if this information is buried in a text paragraph. As a bonus, a table breaks up a gray expanse of text. If tables of data are necessary, for example in a report, these are best placed in an appendix so that they are readily available for reference but do not distract the readers' attention in the text. In contrast, most text tables should be concise summaries (results of the analysis of data), to provide readers with just the information they need and to help you to make a point.

There is an even better way to present numbers, especially if you don't have to show the actual amounts or are working with percentages: make the table into a chart. Charts not only look good on the page, in part because they use colors or differently shaded areas, but they are better than tables at presenting comparisons at a glance.

To create a chart, you first enter the figures into your spreadsheet program and then use the software's automatic chart-creation feature to make the chart. Next, copy and paste the chart into the document.

For example, using the figures from Table 3.5, we can end up with the following chart:

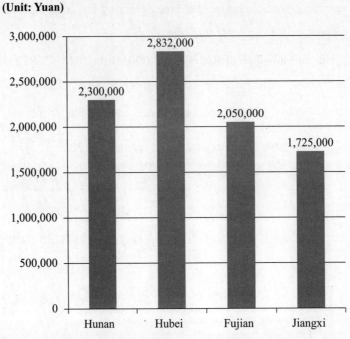

Figure 3.6 Regional sales figures for 2020

Notice that we can see, in an instant, that Hubei had the highest sales figure and Jiangxi the lowest. If you use a chart and cannot present actual values, what do you do with the table? In reports and similar documents, you can put the table in an appendix at the end. Readers who want the actual figures can look there.

Here are a few more guidelines for using graphics in your documents:

- All graphs, charts, pictures, and tables must be identified in some way, usually by a numbered title or caption: Figure 1, Table 1, Picture 1, Chart 1, and so on.
  - ✧ Normally, the title of a table will be on top of the table, while the caption for a graph, chart, photograph, or other illustration will be below. (These illustrations are often called "figures".) If you right-click on a graph, your word processor may offer you the option of creating a caption.
  - ✧ Captions and titles must have a few words identifying what the graphic or table is about, e.g. "Figure 8: Gross and net sales for Hunan, 2019" " Picture 2: Portrait of the artist as a young man, December 1956 (Cartoon by Louis Taylor)".
- All graphs, charts, pictures, tables, and data published elsewhere (digitally or otherwise) should have a source note, e.g. "Data source: US Bureau of Labor Statistics, Current Population Survey, Labor Force Statistics, 2019" or see the "source" notes.

Chapter 3 Document Design

- ✧ The source for a table will usually be placed directly under the table and labeled "Source".

- ✧ For a figure, chart, or other illustration, the credit or source line sometimes appears in the lower right corner underneath the caption, often in a smaller font size than the caption. Sometimes, credit lines for illustrations go in parentheses immediately after the title or caption, e.g. "Picture 2: Portrait of the artist as a young man, December 1956 (Cartoon by Louis Taylor)".

- Tables and graphics must be referred to in the text of the document, e.g. (see Figure 5), (see Table 3), or "as the adjacent photograph shows".

- Don't separate a sentence with a graphic. The full sentence must go before or after the graphic or, better still, around the graphic as a text wrap.

- Don't, unless it's unavoidable, break a table between two pages. Use a separate page for that table and its accompanying text (i.e. its title and any notes, including its source note).

- Keep graphics and text together. That is, don't, unless it's unavoidable, refer in your text—e.g. (see Figure 4.8)—to graphics that are on another page.

- If your graphics take up more than half the page, consider giving them a page to themselves. In this case, of course, your text will be referring to graphics on another page. This works best if the graphics and text are on facing pages.

- Use pie charts and bar graphs to show the relationships between elements. Use line graphs when you want to display a trend, say the price of oil over several decades or a company's sales over six months.

3.7.2 Boxes and Pictures

Boxed text and graphics are easy ways to make your document more attractive. The box can contain additional textual material, called a sidebar. For example:

> **Graphics Tip**
> When presenting numbers, if the actual figures are important, use a table. If the comparison is important, use a chart.

Figure 3.7   An example of boxed text

Another technique for document design is using pull quotes: taking important points out of the text and putting them in a box. For example:

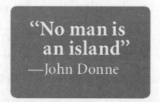

Figure 3.8　An example of pull quotes

Pull quotes can be from the text itself, or they can highlight material that is quoted in the text. In the latter case, it's best to put quotation marks around the quoted text. If you are just quoting from the document text itself, the quotation marks are not necessary. These days, pull quotes are indicated using various methods. For example:

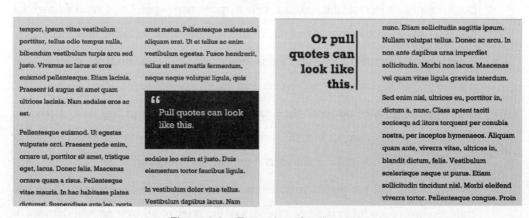

Figure 3.9　Examples of pull quotes

Another attractive option for boxes is to use color, either for the box lines, the text, or both. Or the boxes themselves can be in color with white text. Shading the boxes can also be effective. Or, instead of using a full box, you can have lines on top of and below the boxed text or even to one side of the boxed text.

Finally, in document design, pictures, drawings, cartoons, and photographs enliven a piece of text, if they are appropriate and relevant. Remember that pictures, figures, charts, and the like almost always need captions to identify them, and, again, they need to be pointed to in the text, e.g. (see Picture 12) or (see the following picture) or (see Figure 5).

3.7.3　Drop Capitals

Drop capitals at the start of chapters or sections can also make your pages more attractive. For example:

> Never start a sentence with a numeral. Either write the number out or rewrite the sentence to start with some other words. For example, "2020 sales figures indicate a sharp decline in the fourth quarter" should be rewritten "Sales figures for 2020 indicate a sharp decline in the fourth quarter".

Many word-processing programs will "insert" a drop capital and let you adjust the font style, size, and depth (two lines, three lines, etc.). In general, the larger the heading for the chapter or section, the larger the number of lines the drop cap should take. So, the "Heading 1" style in Word might take a four-line drop cap, "Heading 2" a three-line drop cap, and so on. It never hurts to experiment with different options to see what looks best.

❯ Exercise

Each of the lists below has one or two errors. Identify and correct them.

1) The most important things in life are:
   - Happiness
   - Having good friends
   - Making a good income

2) When you assemble a desk, be sure to do the following
   - Make sure all parts are in the box;
   - Use the correct tools; and
   - Keep your temper

3) My favorite novels are:
   - Wuthering Heights
   - Vanity Fair
   - Tess of the D'Urbervilles

Chapter 4
Writing for Job Opportunities

In a competitive world where one particular job opening may attract dozens or even hundreds of job applicants, it is of great importance for a job seeker to create impressive résumés and effective cover letters to stand out among competitors. Résumés and cover letters are often the first written documents about job seekers that recruiters and employers will read before making decisions. Targeted, customized, and professional résumés and cover letters allow job seekers to highlight the experience and skills that match the employers' needs, thus communicating successfully with possible employers and greatly enhancing the opportunity to make interviews scheduled.

In this chapter, you will learn about:

- highlighting reader-centered communication;
- marketing yourself as a job seeker;
- résumés;
- cover letters.

4.1 Highlighting Reader-centered Communication

Résumés and cover letters are written documents to communicate with potential recruiters and employers. The essence of successful communication in the workplace lies in the reader-centered approach; therefore, to make written communication successful, job seekers need to have an in-depth understanding of the prospective jobs and employers. Résumés and cover letters are to be written to the specific audience and convey specific information that the specific readers need. Furthermore, résumés and cover letters need to be customized for successful communication in different contexts and situations.

4.1.1 Communicating with a Specific Purpose

Researching prospective jobs is often the first stage of the job exploration process and will help you to get to know what specific experiences, skills, abilities, and possible contributions need to be highlighted in the résumés and cover letters. As a job seeker, before writing résumés and cover letters, you need to learn to find the available resources and collect in-depth information for job openings and prospective employers that fit in with your specific objectives.

Chapter 4 Writing for Job Opportunities

To write specifically, you will need to keep in mind the following issues:

- What job openings are available and will best fit your personal career goals?
- How can you make in-depth research on the job openings and prospective employers?
- Who are your specific audience or prospective employers?
- What specific information will the prospective employer expect from your résumé or cover letter?

To get the interview opportunities and find a dream job, it is necessary for you to make in-depth research on job openings and prospective employers and to write specifically for a targeted purpose. In most cases, the following points need to be noted.

Clarify Specific Job-seeking Objectives

You are planning to use your knowledge or skills to serve the prospective company, and make contributions; however, all your knowledge and skills may be useless if you cannot communicate your objectives clearly and efficiently in your résumé or cover letter. To communicate successfully, you need to make a good self-assessment of your objectives and gather in-depth information. To find a dream job in the competitive job market, and to find employers that share your values, you also need to explore job openings and identify companies that may fit in with your field and career goals.

Identify Specific Job Openings

Research is a critical part of the job search process and is an important strategy to make you a more marketable candidate among competitors. The purpose of doing research is to find target employers and develop a list of employers that you might consider sending your résumés and cover letters to. You can use a variety of job search methods to find specific job-seeking resources. You can use job-seeking websites, company websites, various social media sites, search engines for web postings, and other sources to identify job openings catering to your main interests and your secondary interests. For students, on-campus events and career affairs also provide good opportunities for face-to-face communication with employers. Family, friends, classmates, alumni, faculty members, or staff may also offer you potential job opportunities.

Determine Specific Needs of Prospective Employers

It is crucial to understand the potential employers to make your written communication effective. No matter how much you know and how talented you are, your writing strategy should focus on the information that your readers require; extra information will only decrease their work efficiency. It is also important to determine what specific needs your readers require and offer the right information in your résumé and cover letter. Analyzing the specific needs of prospective employers will help to decide what specific details should be part of your writing. The needs of employers could be rather different, but a large majority of employers will look for certain general characteristics when reviewing résumés and cover letters.

4.1.2 Communicating with Customized Designs

Sometimes, you need to customize your résumés or cover letters according to different employers. The customized information you offer to the targeted job openings will influence the decisions of your potential recruiters and employers when they review your résumés and cover letters. Various elements will shape your prospective recruiters and employers; they may consider different factors when they recruit new employees; therefore, in different situations you need to use different ways to present yourself.

As you make research on potential recruiters and employers, you will need to keep in mind the following issues:

- What elements will shape your potential recruiters and employers?
- What kind of customized information should be included in your résumé or cover letter?
- Does your résumé or cover letter tailor to the special backgrounds of the target readers?

To gain maximum response from prospective employers, think constantly about your readers. In most cases, the following points need to be noted.

Identify the Specialty of the Reader

When you write a résumé or cover letter, you may be writing to a wide variety of potential recruiters or employers who may have different educational backgrounds, different levels of familiarity with your major, and different professional concerns and purposes. What you present in your résumé or cover letter will shape the response of potential recruiters and employers while the success of job-related communication depends on their response.

Understand Expectations of the Reader

Your résumé and cover letter will enhance work effectiveness of your prospective employers if you have a good understanding of their expectations and help them to locate the information that they need quickly, easily, and accurately. This will make the communication easier and bring a better response from them. Therefore, the customized information catering to the needs of specific recruiters and employers with different goals and expectations will be required to be included for successful written communication. To help the readers to find the key information quickly, you need to use an easy-to-read writing style and highlight the points that the readers will find.

Consider the Cultural Background of the Reader

Today, the world is getting globalized, and your résumé and cover letter may be read by recruiters and employers from other nations with different ethnic or cultural backgrounds. Therefore, customized information may also be required for successful written communication because the potential recruiters and employers may come from different countries or different cultural backgrounds and may have different values. It is also important for you to look for companies that share your values and resonate with your interests and aspirations.

4.2 Marketing Yourself as a Job Seeker

Besides having effective research and analysis on the prospective jobs and employers, you also need to have an overall assessment of your strengths and to market and sell yourself successfully through written communication. Effective and professional résumés and cover letters are successful personal presentations that will market and advertise job seekers, making them stand out among the competitors. Only applicants who communicate successfully with potential employers and prove to be well-qualified will be chosen for the job.

4.2.1 Assessing Personal Strengths and Usability

Self-assessment is a process required in which you reflect on your strengths and objectives and become aware of your skills, abilities, experiences, interests, values, goals, and aspirations. After researching and understanding how the company or organization functions and what the prospective employer is looking for, job seekers need to select information catering to the needs of the prospective employers.

As you make a self-assessment, you will need to keep in mind the following issues:

- What specific skills, abilities, experiences, and accomplishments can be highlighted in your résumé and cover letter?
- To gain maximum response from prospective recruiters and employers, what possible contributions should be mentioned?
- What personal interests, values, aspirations, or preferences may be mentioned?

To gain maximum response from prospective employers, think constantly about your strengths before writing for job opportunities. In most cases, the following points need to be noted.

Convey Strengths and Usability to the Reader

Making a self-assessment guides you to have a good understanding of yourself and helps you to convey the right information for certain positions. For example, Larry Lee is an engineer with extensive road, subway, and railroad construction experience, but poor writing skills. As he was timid to ask for help to improve and reshape his résumé and cover letter, he lost the opportunity to work for a large construction company. His talents and experience can only be discovered if he can convey his skills and abilities clearly to the reader.

Present Possible Contributions to the Reader

Employers are expecting to hire employees with skills, abilities, and experiences that will help to solve problems and make contributions to the development of the company or organization. Your writing is a way of communication that will persuade your future employers that you have the potential to serve a practical purpose and may make valuable contributions to the company or organization.

Organize Usable Information for the Reader

Self-assessment helps you to identify strengths that can be emphasized in the résumé and cover letter and weaknesses that should be downplayed. Furthermore, it helps you to understand your achievements and your potential for advancement and professional growth. By summarizing your strengths and career goals, you can write with the needs of potential employers in mind. Thus, assessment of your usability, your work values, and aspirations matching the position is an important step before writing.

4.2.2 Presenting and Selling Yourself Through Writing

Effective research and self-assessment smooth the way of collecting and sorting out the information matching the requirements of certain job openings. Besides, job seekers also need to learn to have solid written communication skills to present the tailored information to potential recruiters and employers smartly and professionally.

As you present yourself through written documents, you will need to keep in mind the following issues:

- What makes your résumé and cover letter effective and professional?
- Are your résumé and cover letter persuasive enough to make the employers invite you for an interview?
- What kind of résumé will be the best choice for highlighting your strengths and usability?

To gain maximum response from prospective employers, think constantly about your presentation and design. In most cases, the following points need to be noted.

Prepare Professional Marketing Materials

A solid marketing strategy involves professional writing skills. Failure to create quality marketing materials like your résumé and cover letter will lead to a struggle in the employment process and even make you lose the opportunity of getting an interview. A professional résumé showcases your communication skills and presents customized information indicating your strengths which will benefit the company. A cover letter helps you to introduce yourself to prospective employers and create a connection with the employment opportunities.

Produce Maximum Response from Readers

To gain maximum response from prospective employers, you should choose the kind of résumé that will showcase your strengths and usability most persuasively. Usually, there are the reverse chronological résumé, the functional résumé, and the combination résumé, and each kind of résumé has its special way of presenting yourself. A well-targeted cover letter highlighting your fit for the position and introducing your key qualifications to those who will be conducting the candidate search process is also necessary.

Write for Action

Successful résumés and cover letters are bridges between you and employers and establish a possible relationship between you and the job openings. You are using your writing to influence your readers and arouse their curiosity in your potential and thus make an action to offer you an invitation for an interview. Thus, action verbs like *accomplished*, *organized*, *enlisted*, *evaluated* are often used in the résumé to call for action.

4.3 Résumés

A résumé is a written document about one to two pages long, listing and summarizing your professional background, including your education, work experience, qualifications, and skills for marketing or selling yourself as a job applicant. Recruiters and employers depend on résumés to screen potential employees and decide whether they are qualified for the open positions.

For an applicant, a résumé is a written document used to advertise the usability and communicate with prospective employers for the target of getting an interview. Depending on the field, applicants apply for different positions. For example, if you are in the field of economics, you may apply for positions, such as accountant, loan officer, and credit controller. If you are in the area of marketing, you may apply for positions, such as sales manager, market analyst, and market assistant. If you are in the area of computer science, you may apply for positions, such as computer programmer, information system administrator, and software engineer. And if you are in the area of art, you may apply for positions, such as animation designer, painter, and so on.

As you present yourself through résumés, you will need to keep in mind the following issues:

- What job title are you looking for?
- Which type of résumé will be a good choice for your application?
- What should be emphasized in résumé writing to apply for jobs concerning various industries?
- What relevant information can showcase your qualifications and capabilities for the job?

4.3.1 Basic Types of Résumés

There are various types of résumés for you to choose: the reverse chronological résumé, the functional résumé, the combination résumé, the non-traditional résumé, the mini résumé, the curriculum vitae, and so on. Most résumés include the following basic information: contact information, career objective and résumé summary, experience or employment history, skills, and education. And choosing the right type of résumé will improve your chances of landing an interview for your dream job.

As expected, there is no single form or standard for a résumé that will meet the needs of all people for all jobs, so you should prepare to create more than one résumé along the path of your job hunting. The reverse chronological résumé, the functional résumé, and the combination résumé are the most common types of résumés for your job application. The following discussion will focus on them.

4.3.2 The Reverse Chronological Résumé

The reverse chronological résumé is the most common type of résumé which lists your information in reverse chronological order. Your personal information is listed in descending order with the most recent items appearing at the very beginning, and each job experience is followed up with a specific description of your duties, accomplishments, and skills in the specific position.

The reverse chronological résumé is the most traditional type of résumé and is still the most popular type being used today. Employers typically prefer the reverse chronological résumé simply because it is the most recognizable résumé and it works well for the job applicant with solid work experience. By listing data and information in reverse chronological order, the reverse chronological résumé allows employers to quickly locate information about your recent work experience and accomplishments.

The following is an example:

Heidi Lee

Room 2121, No. 89, Zhongshan Road

Xiamen, Fujian Province, China 360008

Phone:13606662122

Email: Heidilee@internet.com

(Continued)

Objective	Brand Manager
Summary	Eight years of brand management experience, including marketing, branding, and product management skills in the hospitality and tourism sectors. Proficient in conducting extensive market and consumer research and drafting brand and product marketing proposals, also in conducting relevant marketing activities and the development of new products.
Key skills	• Brand Management • Sales Promotion • Market Research
Professional experience	**Haixi Travel Agency, Xiamen, Fujian, August 2019–Present** Brand Manager • Strategically planned and successfully reached a 70% increase in sales revenue through complete brand ownership. • Organized a marketing budget plan of $8 million for brand management and new product marketing. **Huashen Travel Agency, Zhangzhou, Fujian, January 2017–July 2019** Sales Manager • Conducted research on consumer trends by building a database for mining consumption development trends, data analysis, etc. • Created communication plans and organized campaigning activities for Round Earth Building travel package promotion. • Performed Round Earth Building marketing initiatives through the newspaper, radio, internet, and other channels. **Xiashun Hotel, Fuzhou, Fujian, January 2015–December 2016** Market Researcher • Collaborated with the sales and marketing team to conduct research on Fujian provincial hotel service statistics and analyze marketing initiatives through analysis. • Worked with regional managers to create marketing proposals based on market research.

(Continued)

	• Liaised with the Sales Department for the feasibility of marketing plans and coordinated with the Legal Department for claims & partnerships with other relevant hotels and travel agencies.
Education	**Boston University, Boston, September 2012–May 2014** M.A. in Tourism Management **Tsinghua University, Beijing, September 2008–July 2012** B.A. in Economic Management
Languages	English, French, Japanese

The reverse chronological résumé is the most advantageous when you have several years of professional experience. Your career progression has been steady and preferably in one industry, and you don't have gaps in employment. However, it is not suitable for job seekers who do not have a concrete and continuous career path and even have taken many breaks in the career development journey.

A typical reverse chronological résumé usually consists of the following sections: name, contact information, career objective, résumé summary, professional experience, education, skills, and additional sections (e.g. awards and honors, achievements, certifications, interests, references). The layout of such a résumé is not fixed and can be very versatile. For example, if you have rich professional experience, you should put work experience first. However, if you're a recent college graduate, you should put education first. You can prioritize the parts of your résumé based on your strengths and experience. Remember to make sure the entries in each section follow the reverse chronological order.

Let's make a closer study of each of these sections in a reverse chronological résumé one by one.

The Name and Contact Information

Your name should always be listed on top of the first page of your résumé no matter what type of résumé you prepare. It is usually highlighted with a larger font or boldface. List your contact information right beneath your name and the information should be current, listing your mailing address, telephone or cell phone number, email address, and a professional website address if you have one. As a group of information, the name and the contact information are usually centered or left-justified.

The following is an example with the name and contact information centered:

Mary Durst
19019 Home Blvd. • Regina, OR 00166 • (666) 666–1010 • mary.durst@email.com

The following is an example with the name and contact information left-justified:

Cody Fredrickson
Baton Rouge LA • (123) 456–7891
cfredrickson@email.com

The Career Objective and the Résumé Summary

The career objective and the résumé summary can be listed separately or as a whole, giving the recruiter a glimpse into your résumé profile, stating what you want, and emphasizing what skills and qualifications you have.

The following is an example of a job seeker looking for a job as an engineering manager with the objective and summary listed as a whole:

Engineering Manager

Building better-performing companies and products through engineering.

Respected engineer with more than 10 years of experience in engineering and management, research and development, leadership and mentoring, as well as problem-solving, seeks position with a top firm.

Key skills include:
- Conducting Six Sigma Projects
- Reducing Warranty Costs
- Experience in Engine Control
- Performing Custom Data Acquisition
- Experience with NVH Testing Systems
- Improving Product Quality and Manufacturability

The following is an example of a job seeker looking for a job as a market analyst with the objective and summary listed separately:

Chapter 4   Writing for Job Opportunities

Career Objective

Market intelligence analyst looking for an opportunity to work with senior management to develop corporate marketing plans and enhance branding goals.

Core Qualifications

Experience with database software, spreadsheet software, order processing systems, and content management systems.

Professional Experience

    This is the heart and mind of a reverse chronological résumé and is often read carefully by the recruiter. The professional experience showcases your current and previous work experience. In this section, the dates you worked, the job title, and the name of the company for each position you held will be listed clearly by following the reverse chronological order. The location of the company can also be listed. Bullet points instead of paragraphs are often used to list the experience, focusing on presenting. Action words, such as *supervised*, *achieved*, *partnered*, *managed*, *boosted* are often used to start bullet points to achieve a better effect.

    The following is an example of the professional experience of a senior financial analyst:

Professional Experience

TradeLot, Senior Financial Analyst   **July 2019–Present**

- Functions as a broker between the company's corporate finance and regional operations departments.
- Prepares financial results versus budget analysis of spending with a focus on performance in key areas.
- Responds to ad hoc requests for financial information from 17 operations personnel as needed.
- Reconciles accrued expense and advance payment balance sheet accounts for assigned business units to ensure financial continuity per unit.

Cloud Clearwater, Financial Analyst   **August 2017–June 2019**

- Updated all renovation-project spreadsheets to new commitments and monitored expenditures for budget compliance.
- Analyzed and reported variances on overtime expenditures by comparing payroll's

(Continued)

> Overtime Differential Report versus approved Overtime Requests, resulting in 33% cost savings.
> - Provided ongoing education and management consulting to ensure that all 77 stakeholders properly understood reports, methodologies, systems, and source data.

Education

Your education communicates your value to the employer. It can be listed below or above the experience section, depending on how much experience you have. The education section starts with your highest degree and goes backward in reverse chronological order. The university name, the graduation year, the degree, and the major or specialized field of study will be included. If you're fresh out of school, you may consider adding information on GPA, the relevant coursework, the honors, or other relevant information.

The following is an example:

> **EDUCATION**
>
> **Auburn University**, M.B.A. in Finance, 2018
> **University of Costa Rica**, Bachelor of Arts in Business Economics, 2004

Skills

The relevant skills you possess will be listed here. Soft skills, hard skills, as well as other skills which are relevant to the job can be listed.

The following is an example of a job seeker applying for a job as a dentist:

> **SKILLS**
>
> Dental assistant skills include: DANB certification • X-ray certification • Sterilizing and maintaining dentistry equipment • Managing appointments • Preparing dental filling materials • Minor oral surgery experience • Patient communication

Additional Sections

The relevant information listed in the additional sections (you can also use the headline like "Added Value" "Honors and Awards" "Additional Skills" "Volunteer/Community Service", etc. to show your additional skills, achievements, values) earns you extra points and boosts your chances of getting an interview.

4.3.3 The Functional Résumé

The functional résumé is skills-based and is a type of résumé format that primarily showcases the skills of the job seeker. A functional résumé is a good choice if you want to feature your skills rather than your experience. As opposed to the reverse chronological résumé, the functional résumé highlights skills and abilities and organizes information of a job seeker according to the importance of skills and abilities, placing core competences and areas of expertise first, before listing experience and other necessary information. It emphasizes the functions or skills of a job seeker while de-emphasizing when or where the functions and skills were used.

The functional résumé works best for job seekers with diverse but unrelated work experience. It is also a good choice if you are a recent graduate who does not have extensive professional experience but has gained significant skills through academic study and research in the university. You can also choose to use this type of résumé if you have been changing jobs or have significant gaps in your employment history, and thus do not have significant experience relevant to the job you apply for. In short, if your qualifications are better categorized under types of skills rather than your work experience, a functional résumé will be an appropriate choice.

The following is an example:

James Kennedy

555 Cherry Lane

Ann Arbor, Michigan 48111–9626

111–777–8888

jameskennedy@email.com

Summary

Customer Service Representative with over three years of experience resolving complex customer inquiries. Passionate about building strong customer relationships, driving brand loyalty, and increasing customer engagement.

Area of Experience

Retail Sales, Data Entry, Microsoft Office, Typing, Complaint Resolution, Service-based Selling, Fluency in French and Spanish.

(Continued)

Skills

Process Streamlining

Created customer service email scripts used across the company to interact with customers. Single-handedly created the customer service representative training manual, reducing the onboarding process from 8 to 6 weeks. Reduced average customer representative call time by 90 seconds with intuitive online training.

Complaint Resolution

Answered an average of 50+ calls per day from unsatisfied customers related to delays in shipment, order mistakes, and lost orders. Achieved an average customer satisfaction rate of 97%, exceeding the team target by 12%.

Service-based Selling

Consistently exceeded application targets by 10%+ with innovative up-selling techniques. Pioneered development of an improved system for following up with unsatisfied customers, reducing the customer churn rate by 6%.

Experience

Cloud Clearwater, 2017

Customer Service Manager: Managed customer relationships via the phone and email to obtain payments and resolve inquiries. Customer referral program: A spearheaded project, increasing the customer base by 15% in less than 6 months.

TradeLot, 2016

Customer Service Representative: Resolved customer inquiries via the phone and email, consistently exceeding targets and pioneering processes for better customer satisfaction.

Education

Coral Springs University, 2009–2013

Bachelor of Science in Business Administration

A typical functional résumé usually consists of the following sections: name and job title, contact information, summary, skills, work experience, education, and additional section. The design of a functional résumé focuses on skills and qualifications. Let's make a closer study of each of these sections in a functional résumé one by one.

The Name and Job Title

If you are professional and your qualifications and skills match with the position or job title you are applying for, you can list job titles like "Sales Manager" "Animation Designer" "Civil Engineer", right under your name. However, if you are using a functional résumé to switch roles or industries, the job title should be omitted because it could divert the attention or even confuse the recruiter.

The following is an example:

Heidi Chen
Animation Designer

Contact Information

No matter what type of résumé you choose, the contact information is a must and to be listed with the address, phone number, email, and social media accounts (if necessary) so that the prospective employers can get in touch with you.

The following is an example:

Heidi Lee
221 West Sunshine Road
Xiamen, Fujian Province, China 361009
H: 221–362–2221
M: 221–121–2121
Heidilee@163.com

The Summary

The functional résumé uses the summary (you can also use the headlines like "Qualification Summary" "Professional Profile", etc.) to highlight the core skills or qualifications. However, long, boring, and irrelevant skills or qualifications would reduce your chances of an interview, so it is important to emphasize your competences and achievements gained from your work and educational history which are relevant to the position.

The following is an example:

Summary

Exceptionally well-organized and professional with more than six years' experience and a solid academic background in accounting and financial management; excellent analytical and problem-solving skills; able to handle multiple projects while producing high-quality work in a fast-paced, deadline-oriented environment.

Skills

The skills section (you can also use the headlines like "Relevant Skills" "Professional Accomplishments", etc.) is the shining part of your functional résumé. Three to four professional skills can be categorized like "Sales and Marketing Experience" "Foreign Language Fluency" and "Team Building and Leadership Expertise". Under each of the categorized skills, list two to three bullets detailing professional experience and accomplishments relating to the respective skill. The specific information listed will make your communication successful.

The following is an example:

Skills

Accounting and Financial Management

- Developed and maintained accounting records for up to 50 bank accounts.
- Formulated monthly and year-end financial statements and generated various payroll records, including federal and state payroll reports, annual tax reports, W-2 and 1099 forms, etc.
- Tested accuracy of account balances and prepared supporting documentation for submission during a comprehensive three-year audit of financial operations.
- Formulated intricate pro forma budgets.
- Calculated and implemented depreciation/amortization schedules.

Information Systems Analysis and Problem-solving

- Computerized accounting systems for two organizations.
- Analyzed and successfully reprogrammed software to meet customer requirements.
- Researched and corrected problems to assure effective operation of new computerized systems.

Work Experience

The work experience section (you can also use the headlines like "Professional Experience" "Work History", etc.) of functional résumés is typically brief since you're trying to guide the recruiters to focus on your applicable skills. In this section, you showcase your experience without a prominent display of it to shift the focus on the skills and other qualifications, simply listing the positions held along with company names, locations, and employment dates in the reverse chronological order.

The following is an example:

Work Experience
Sales Associate & Machinist Assistant, Precision Tool, Omaha, NE (2021 to present)
Market Research, Mutual of Omaha, Omaha, NE (Fall Semester, 2020)

Education

In the education section, list your highest degree and most relevant certificates with the name of the university, the location, the degree received, and the date you graduated along with your GPA (if necessary). Highlight your educational experience corresponding to the job you are applying for and in case your degree is not relevant to the position, try to keep this section short. The headline "Education" can be replaced by "Training and Education" to incorporate more relevant skills gained from training programs.

The following is an example:

Bachelor of Science, Bellevue University, Bellevue, NE (June, 2020)
Major: Computer Information Systems in Business
Minor: Mathematics
Graduated with Professional Honors
GPA: 3.78/4.00

Additional Section

The additional section (you can also use the headlines like "Added Value" "Honors and Awards" "Additional Skills" "Volunteer/Community Service", etc.) is optional. It showcases additional information that improves your opportunities of getting hired once you have grasped the attention of the recruiter. Awards, distinctions, and extracurricular activities helping you to stand out can be added in this section.

The following is an example:

Added Value

Proficient in MS Office (Word, Excel, PowerPoint, Outlook), QuickBooks

Basic Knowledge of MS Access, SQL, Visual Basic, C++

4.3.4 The Combination Résumé

A combination résumé is also called a chrono-functional résumé. It is a type of résumé which combines formatting characteristics of the reverse chronological résumé and the functional résumé. It highlights both the job seeker's key skills and employment history. Usually, it begins with a description of skills and qualifications, followed by a concise description of the job seeker's reverse chronological employment history.

A combination résumé is a good choice for a job seeker with solid experience in a certain industry. It is also suitable for a job seeker with a consistent job history to showcase consistency while emphasizing the most valuable skills. For job seekers who have gaps in their employment history or who want to prepare a résumé for a career change, it is also a good choice. New graduates or students with a fairly short employment history can also choose to use this type of résumé.

The following is a combination résumé of a job seeker with solid experience in the computer industry:

Christian Hybrid

IT Manager

christian.w.hybrid@gmail.com

202–555–0177

Skills Summary

Programming and App Development

- Developed and built 20+ mobile apps and 30+ websites providing exceptional user experience.
- Named BCD M&E's "Top Programmer of the Year" for three consecutive years 2009–2011.
- 15+ years' experience in C, C++, Cocoa, and Objective-C.

(Continued)

- C Certified Professional Programmer (2006), C++ Certified Professional Programmer (2009).

Leadership

- 8+ years' experience in team management (teams of 10–50 colleagues) and project coordination.
- Designed and implemented a new IT management model with Apple's New York Branch, increasing the quarterly productivity by 33% and resulting in an increase in employee satisfaction.
- Trained and mentored 50+ junior developers for certification exams (88% success rate).

Business Management

- Coordinated 20+ projects with a budget of over $200,000.
- Optimized procurement processes to reduce BCD M&E's annual costs by 27%.
- Successfully cooperated with sales and marketing teams on new business strategies which helped increase Apple New York's sales volume by 23%.

Additional Skills

- Adobe Photoshop—Excellent
- InDesign—Excellent
- CRM Platforms—Advanced
- Google Analytics—Advanced

Experience

IT Manager

Apple, New York City, NY

2013–Present

- Supervised the IT team in creating mobile apps providing the best user experience for Apple's customers all over the world.
- Developed, reviewed, and tested innovative and visionary new applications using emerging technologies.
- Guided talent that provides technical support and training while working in partnership with the business team.

(Continued)

Senior IT Specialist

BCD M&E, New York City, NY

2006–2013

- Developed, reviewed, and tested websites for internal and external stakeholders; led innovation in mobile applications.
- Cooperated with procurement teams in optimizing procurement processes.

Software Engineer

Oracle, Redwood City, CAFCB Global, New York City, NY

2003–2006

Education

M.S. in Computer Science, Cum Laude

The City College of New York, New York City, NY

2002

B.S. in Computer Science

University of California, Berkeley, CA

2000

The following is another example of a combination résumé. This résumé belongs to someone with no paid job experience, and even so, the writer effectively conveys information about her skills, increasing her odds of winning interviews. As with other examples of résumés provided, each of the jobs and duties listed begins with an action word.

Shirley Marshall

12344 Vine Street

Tucson, AZ, 85725

(510)–555–1234

Email: SMarshall7@test.net

Summary

Dependable, skilled General Office Worker with over ten years of transferable experience. Proven communication, clerical, and customer service skills in a variety of settings. Positive, personable attitude with a history of producing quality results and satisfied

(Continued)

customers. Computer literate.

Selected Skills

General Office

- Scheduled appointments.
- Paid invoices and maintained accurate financial records.
- Answered phones and took messages.
- Organized and implemented meetings efficiently.
- Created documents and prepared reports using WordPerfect and MS Word.

Customer Service

- Welcomed visitors in a friendly, courteous manner.
- Provided clients with desired information in a timely, efficient manner.
- Assisted customers with concerns.
- Established friendly, lasting relationships with the clientele and vendors.

Communication

- Utilized email as an effective tool for communication.
- Answered phones in a professional, courteous manner.
- Demonstrated ability to express ideas and influence action in a team environment.
- Established rapport with diverse groups and individuals.

Related Volunteer Experience

General Office Volunteer	Veterans of Foreign Wars—Tucson, AZ	4 years
Event Coordinator	Neighborhood Watch—Phoenix, AZ	5 years
Elected Secretary	Parent Teachers Association—Phoenix, AZ	6 years
Group/Activities Leader	Boy Scouts of America—Phoenix, AZ	6 years
Family Manager	Self-employed—Phoenix, AZ	8 years

Education

High School Diploma: St. Mary's Catholic High School, Phoenix, AZ

A typical combination résumé is usually sectioned into two parts. The first part is similar to a functional résumé, highlighting skills, achievements, and qualifications, and the second part is a compressed and concise description of employment history. The design of the first part allows the résumé to emphasize the most important elements. Job objectives, significant skills, areas of expertise, and relevant accomplishments will be incorporated according to the importance. The design of the second part presents a reverse chronological employment history, focusing on important work experience relevant to the job position. Additional sections with relevant information like training, education, languages may be added to a combination résumé, depending on the relevance of your experience with the position applied.

Before you make your final decision of choosing the right format for your résumé, let's generalize and compare these résumé structures to see which format is a better choice for you:

Table 4.1　Comparison of résumé structures

The Reverse Chronological Résumé	The Functional Résumé	The Combination Résumé
It highlights your experience and achievements.	It highlights your skills and competences.	It highlights skills relevant to your work history.
It exposes gaps in employment.	It conceals your work experience and employment gaps.	It showcases specialized professional skills.
It is easy to be organized and be consistent in formatting.	It is easy to be creative and has a portfolio with various formats.	It is not so easy to be formatted and organized.

4.4　Cover Letters

A cover letter is a professional document sent together with another main document, such as a résumé, and it serves to introduce the main document to the reader. When you apply for a job, a cover letter is an accompanying document that comes along with your résumé to show why you are the best candidate for the position. It highlights your skills or experiences that are most applicable to the job in a more personal way. If a résumé is a list of skills, experiences, qualifications, and achievements, a cover letter is a written overview of what is on your résumé for marketing yourself.

As you write your cover letter, you will need to keep in mind the following issues:

- What is a good way to create a response-producing cover letter?
- What information should be included in a cover letter?
- What information should be avoided in a cover letter?

Chapter 4   Writing for Job Opportunities

The following is an example of a cover letter:

2582 Lakeview Avenue
Tampa, FL 33607
841–519–1900
TiffanyMorrison@gmail.com

October 22, 2021

Robert Smith
1632 Hanson Street
Bakersfield, California 94301
805–960–5523
RobertSmith@gmail.com

Dear Mr. Smith,

I'm writing to apply for the position of Restaurant Manager at MOD Sequel. I have more than five years of experience managing restaurants and bars, and my professional expertise aligns closely with the responsibilities outlined in your job advertisement.

In my role as Restaurant Manager for Bar Louie, I proved to be an efficient, enthusiastic, and strong leader. My value quickly became apparent to Bar Louie's shareholders after I single-handedly trained and prepared the entire waitstaff for opening night and beyond. Not only did our team meet sales goals each month for the first year, but the down payment for the property was even paid back after the first six months of operating.

MOD Sequel would benefit from my skills in the following areas:
- Eye for excellence and a high level of standards
- Strong work ethic and leadership skills
- Positive attitude even under pressure

I believe MOD Sequel will be a great success for many years to come, and my extensive expertise will help ensure future success of your establishment. My time spent in this industry has prepared me for such an opportunity, and I sincerely hope I can contribute soon

(Continued)

> as a member of your team.
>
> It would be a privilege to discuss your Restaurant Manager position in more detail. I'm happy to come by whenever it's most convenient for you. Thank you for your time, and I'm looking forward to hearing from you.
>
> Sincerely,
> *Tiffany Morrison*
> Tiffany Morrison

The cover letter is a formal business letter, so the format is the same as a business letter. A typical cover letter usually consists of the following sections: the return address, the date, the inside address, the salutation, the introduction, the body paragraph(s), the closing paragraph, and the signature.

The Return Address

The writer's return address includes the complete mailing address. But, if a letter is printed on the paper with the organization's letterhead, there is no need to repeat the address here. If there is no letterhead, then a return address is needed. For example:

> 1218 Vincent ST
> Lincoln, NE 61201–2316

The Date

The date is placed below the return address. The month should be spelled in full, for example "May 24, 2022".

The Inside Address

The inside address is placed below the date, and gives the recipient's name, position or title (if any), company name, and complete mailing address. For example:

> Mrs. Sophia Stevens
> Hiring Manager
> Sunshine Company

(Continued)

> 21 North Parkway
> Green Meadow Road, NY 11551

The Salutation

The salutation is a professional greeting addressing the hiring manager or the person who is responsible for the recruiting process. Addressing the individual by name creates a connection between you and the reader. For example:

> Dear Mrs. Stevens

If it is impossible to get the name of the hiring manager or the person who is responsible for the recruiting process, greetings relating to the specific job title and the department like "Dear Hiring Manager" "Dear Sales & Marketing Director" "Dear Customer Services Manager" "Dear Vice President" can be used.

The Introduction

It is also called the opening paragraph which is an attention-grabbing paragraph to introduce yourself directly and straightforwardly and clearly states your intention to apply for the position and make the employer know that you are a well-qualified candidate for the job. Your cover letter opening should contain a self-introduction and mention where you found the job posting, and why you want to apply for the job. For example:

> Your recent job posting on your website for a Sales Manager has captured my serious interest. As a dynamic sales manager with over 21 years of professional experience executing sales management, analyzing the sales market, and leading professional teams, I am confident that I would be a valuable asset to Sunshine Company. In response to your job opening, I have attached a résumé that details my professional experience that closely matches your job requirements.

The Body Paragraph(s)

The body paragraph(s) is (are) also called as the middle paragraph(s). This part details your professional experience, skills and qualifications, achievements, and education responding directly to the job description of the position. To include exact words and phrases from the job descriptions in the cover letter will help the prospective employer to feel you are a well-qualified candidate. A bulleted list of your accomplishments can be included, and you can also explain your reasons for desiring the position. For example:

> Some of my key skills that are relevant to this opportunity include:
> - over 21 years of professional experience in a sales management position with a reputation as a resourceful problem-solver for sales promotion of education facilities and equipment;
> - rich experience in providing support and assistance to data management, marketing survey, research, and report writing on projects relating to education facilities and equipment;
> - a comprehensive working knowledge of drafting correspondence, making professional presentations, organizing meetings, negotiating on business projects, traveling for business;
> ...

The Closing Paragraph

The purpose of this part is a call to action. You can restate your interest in the position and your enthusiasm for using your skills to make a contribution to the company or organization and remember to thank the reader for his or her consideration of your application, and end by stating that you're looking forward to the opportunity to further discuss the position. For example:

> If you are looking for a motivated administrative assistant who is committed to the highest standards of work performance, I would welcome the opportunity to meet with you for an in-depth discussion. I am available for an interview at your earliest convenience; please contact me via the phone or email to arrange a time and date for us to meet. Thank you for your time and consideration and I'm looking forward to speaking with you soon.

The Signature

This section ends the letter. For example:

> Sincerely,
>
> Eric Lee

Chapter 4 Writing for Job Opportunities

> **Exercises**

1. *The following is a template for a reverse chronological résumé. Write a résumé for Li Xiaoming for applying for a job as an assistant professor in AAA Foreign Language University.*

Your Name Job Title	**Summary**
Contact Information Address Phone Email	**Work History**
Skills	
Languages	
	Education
	Accomplishments
	References References are available upon request.

2. **Use the following template to write a cover letter.**

> Your Street Address
> City, Province, Zip Code
>
> Date of Letter
>
> Contact Name
> Contact Title
> Company Name
> Street Address
> City, Province, Zip Code
>
> Dear _____,
>
> Opening Paragraph:
>
> Middle Paragraph(s):
>
> Closing Paragraph:
>
> Sincerely,
>
> Your name typed
> Enc.: Résumé

3. **Cover letters can be sent via emails. The following is a template of email for a cover letter. Please try to write a cover letter with the template.**

> **Subject Line of Email Message**
> The subject line always summarizes briefly and clearly the contents of the message.
>
> **Salutation**
> In most emails, a quick greeting is needed to acknowledge the reader before the reader

(Continued)

dives into your main message or request, for example "Dear Mr. or Ms. + Last Name" or "Dear Hiring Manager".

Body

The body of an email is the most important part of your message, and it must have a clear and specific purpose. Several paragraphs can be written for a detailed and specific discussion of the message that you want to deliver. The first paragraph of your letter should include information on why you are writing. Be clear and direct. For example, if you are applying for a job, mention the job title. If you want an informational interview, state that in your opening sentences. The middle paragraph usually describes what you have to provide to the employer or if you're writing to ask for help, and what type of assistance you are seeking. The final paragraph is to conclude your cover letter by thanking the employer for considering you for the position or your connection for helping with your job search.

Closing

Just as you want to start things off on the right foot with your greeting, you also want to part well. That means writing a friendly sign-off, for example "Sincerely,".

Email Signature

First Name + Last Name

Email Address

Phone Number

Chapter 5
Basic Correspondence

Business letters, memos, and emails are important ways of communication in the workplace and should be written professionally with persuasive strategies. Persuasive strategies are vital to successful correspondence writing and will make your business letters, memos, and emails stand out in this competitive workplace and business circle. Good ideas can be neglected and good products may not be sold successfully simply because the messages delivered through business correspondence aren't persuasive or effective enough to be noticed and accepted.

In this chapter, you will learn about:

- writing persuasive messages;
- conveying good news, neutral news, and bad news;
- business letters;
- memos;
- emails.

5.1 Writing Persuasive Messages

Whether you are writing business letters, memos, or emails, you are speaking to your readers' needs and writing with an attempt to convince the readers to do something. To persuade your readers and achieve your goal, you need to market your ideas, plans, products, and services, and show the value of taking action.

As you write professional correspondence in the workplace, you will need to keep in mind the following issues:

- How can you persuade readers to accept your point of view through writing?
- How can you outline the structure of a persuasive message?
- How do you stand out among large quantities of business letters, memos, and emails transmitted every day in the workplace?

5.1.1 Write with the AIDA Model

The AIDA model stands for Attention, Interest, Desire, and Action. The first "A" means to attract attention, "I" means to maintain interest, "D" means to create desire, and the second "A" means to get action. The AIDA model was developed in 1898 by St. Elmo Lewis. Although Lewis's work was primarily focused on helping the personal selling process, it was avidly taken up by marketing and advertising theorists over the next half century.

There are situations when readers tend to refuse your idea, plan, request, or others. The AIDA formula will be a good model for you to learn. It helps to write persuasive messages relating to basic business correspondence. The following is a detailed explanation about AIDA applied in writing basic business correspondence.

Attract Readers' Attention

To attract your readers' attention, you should try to convince the readers right at the start of your writing, and begin with a brief opening statement by demonstrating features, advantages, and benefits catering to the needs of your readers.

Maintain Readers' Interest

To maintain your readers' interest, you should continue your topic with a detailed and specific message, and try to arouse the readers' interest to go on reading with messages relevant to them.

Create Readers' Desire

To create the readers' desire to accept your idea, you should emphasize how the readers will benefit from taking action. For example, in business letters asking a company to join a charity service, you can emphasize how the service will do good to the community. In memos or emails asking for financial support for a project, you can emphasize how the readers will benefit from the support.

Make Readers Get Action

To make your readers get action, you can repeat the main benefits that will be realized from taking action. You should also describe the request specifically to make the readers clear about the action to be taken.

The following is an example, in which the writer is using the AIDA model to write a business letter with persuasive messages:

249 5th Avenue
Pittsburgh, PA 15222

March 30, 2021

Lorraine Thelian
Senior Partner
Ketchum
6 PPG Place
Pittsburgh, PA 15222

Dear Ms. Thelian,

As PNC begins its integration of National City, making it the fifth largest bank in the nation, we are in dire need of an experienced and reliable public relations firm to negotiate the transition. As two companies founded in the Pittsburgh area, we certainly know the importance of growing business on a global level while continuing to grow our local community. We believe that Ketchum is poised to do exactly that—provide the bank with superior media relations and internal communications during this hectic time.

Even though your offices now span the globe, Ketchum's roots in Pittsburgh enable you to understand the core mission of this acquisition. We want to provide current PNC customers and new National City customers with a seamless transition, as well as reassure National City's clients that they are not losing the superior customer service and banking products they received at their community bank. Even though PNC has stepped from a regional to a national bank, our commitment to customer service is unwavering, and we will continue to provide the same excellent services to our current and new customers.

Ketchum will play a vital role in this process. Through a strategic combination of your skilled professionals and our in-house communication staff, we are certain that we can successfully communicate this mission to the Pittsburgh community. In addition, your recent Silver Anvil award is a great testament to the quality of your PR programs and makes us very excited about the potential of working together on this campaign.

(Continued)

> At your earliest convenience, please send me your rate quotes and summary of services. If you could also send a brief history of your partnerships with clients in the financial sector, I would greatly appreciate it. Lorraine, thank you for your time, and I'm looking forward to speaking with you in person.
>
> Sincerely,
> *Lia DeStio*
> Lia DeStio
> PNC Financial Services Group

5.1.2 The Process of Creating Persuasive Messages

Processes, namely planning, compiling, and completing persuasive messages are involved in creating persuasive messages in writing business correspondence.

Plan Persuasive Messages

Before writing persuasive messages, you need to make a good situation analysis and ask yourself what motivates your readers, what benefits your readers might gain from accepting your ideas or taking action in responding to your messages. You also need to collect information of your readers, understanding their interests and concerns. Furthermore, you need to be clear about your relationship with the readers, and clarify your writing purpose and the specific action you want the readers to take.

Compile Persuasive Messages

Writing with an appropriate tone and language in combination with the AIDA model is a good strategy when you compile persuasive messages for business letters, memos, and emails. Firstly, remember to use an opening that attracts the readers' attention and directly states the benefits to your readers. Secondly, offer a strong argument with detailed and convincing evidence in the middle which helps to establish a need and show how to meet it. Thirdly, use facts, statistics, cases, etc. to help the readers to understand what you're discussing, trying to address possible obstacles and offer solutions to prospective obstacles. Finally, end with confident closing that asks for a reasonable action, encouraging a prompt response with your contact information like email addresses, websites, or other options.

Complete Persuasive Messages

After you finish writing persuasive messages, it is important to ensure your writing to be professional with a clear appearance. You need to evaluate the contents of the messages to clarify the information presented, making sure that your writing follows a clear, logical pattern and that you have provided a complete explanation that speaks to your readers' motivations. You need to check the appropriate use of a sincere tone with a good choice of words and easy-to-read sentences with good transitions to tie ideas together. Remember to correct the grammar, punctuation, spelling, and keyboarding mistakes, and make sure the format and design of the business letters, memos, or emails that you are writing are consistent and effective.

5.2 Conveying Good News, Neutral News, and Bad News

Business correspondence can be classified according to the content or message. There are usually good news, neutral news, bad news business letters, memos, and emails. If you want your readers to understand and accept the information you're conveying, you need to learn to be sensitive to your reader's psychology as you write professional correspondence. Good news and neutral news business letters, memos, and emails are easier to write because you are not conveying an unfavorable message; however, bad news letters have to be written carefully to avoid offending your reader with an unfavorable message.

To communicate successfully, you will need to keep in mind the following issues:

- How does psychological understanding relate to communication in basic correspondence writing?
- How can you convey good news?
- How can you convey neutral news?
- How can you convey bad news?

5.2.1 Conveying Good News

Most of the business letters, memos, and emails that you will write in the workplace involve giving good news. Good news business letters, memos, and emails convey good or favorable messages like promotion, salary increase, sales announcement, financial support, or sign of a contract. Although it is easy for your readers to accept favorable messages psychologically, a proper way to write good news business letters, memos, and emails helps you to make a positive impact on your readers.

Usually, a direct approach is the best choice for writing good news business letters, memos, and emails. You can start directly with the good news politely and positively, move directly to your main point, give supporting details, explanation, and commentary with clear organization, and finally conclude by reiterating your main point politely and positively with a note of thanks or congratulations or a call for action.

The following is an example of a good news memo:

MEMORANDUM

To: Southern Communications Employees
From: Brynn Hobbs, CEO
Date: October 6, 2020
Subject: Recruiting Reward Policy

A new policy for rewarding those who recruit potential employees has been adopted by the Human Resources Department. The new policy becomes effective from today and you should take advantage of it, as you would be helping the company as well as yourself.

The new policy is designed to help attract qualified accounting, computer, and communication professionals, which is something that our organization has struggled with recently. To solve the problem, the Human Resources Department has created a "Most Wanted" list of positions needed. Those of you who can successfully recruit an individual to fill a position on the list will receive a $2,500 cash bonus.

To earn the bonus, you must:
- Complete a Recruitment Bonus Request before any communication occurs between the recruit and the company. This form will identify important information, such as the recruit's name, current position, and qualifications.
- Sign the form, have the recruit sign it, and then have the recruiting director sign it.

(Continued)

> - Make sure the form is complete and signed. Once signed by the recruiting director, the form will be submitted to the Human Resources Department.
>
> The "Most Wanted" list will be updated weekly by the recruiting director, so you will always know which positions are needed. Your involvement in this new system will be greatly appreciated. If anybody has any questions or concerns, feel free to call or email me, or contact the Human Resources Department.

5.2.2　Conveying Neutral News

Neutral news business letters, memos, and emails usually convey a neutral message, which does not provoke emotion, containing neither good nor bad news from the perspective of the readers, for example to confirm receiving of a letter, to announce the change of office hours, to place an order, or to make a routine request for information. Care should be taken to write them properly so that the readers will show interest and respond to your message. Similarly, a direct approach is the best choice. You can start directly with the news in a polite way, move directly to your main point, give supporting details, explanation, and commentary with clear organization, and finally conclude by reiterating your main point politely with a note of thanks or a call for action.

The following is an example of conveying neutral news. You are ordering a part for your fridge, you've done some research on the internet, and you know exactly what part you need. The first paragraph of your letter should say something like this: "I would like to place an order for a fridge element, Part # 443–T, for a Haier Model 321 fridge." Then give the details of where you want the fridge part sent, and provide any additional contact information if necessary. If you don't give enough details, such as the part number, the company will have to get back to you. Finally, you can conclude your letter by reiterating your purpose politely with a note of thanks.

5.2.3　Conveying Bad News

Bad news business letters, memos, and emails convey a bad or unfavorable message like a decision on stopping funding for a project, rejection of a job application, denial of a promotion, or rejection of a request. Respect and politeness are required when writing bad news business letters, memos, and emails. Since the way you present negative information can have a substantial impact on the readers, the indirect approach is a tactful writing strategy to avoid offending the readers.

By using the indirect approach, negative information can be embedded in secondary positions. You can start politely and professionally by placing positive or neutral information in front of negative information, outline the details of the issue by providing objective reasons, facts, and supporting evidence, state the decision or the bad or unfavorable news with an explanation of the reasons behind the decision, and close politely and professionally. The readers' hopes and feelings should be respected and considered so that your readers will understand that a firm decision based on objective facts and reasons has been made.

The following is an example of a bad news email:

Dear Mr. Waters,

We're happy to learn that you are enjoying the use of the Sako copier you've been leasing for the past 10 months. Like our many customers, you have discovered that Sako copiers offer remarkable versatility and reliability.

One of the reasons we're able to offer these outstanding copiers at such low leasing rates and equally low purchase prices is that we maintain a slim profit margin. If our program included a provision for applying lease payments toward the purchase price, our overall prices would have to be higher.

Although lease payments cannot be credited toward the purchase price, we can offer you other Sako models that are within your price range. The Sako 400 delivers the same reliability with nearly as many features as the Sako 600.

Please let us demonstrate the Sako 400 to your staff in your office, Mr. Waters. Our representative, Tracy Wilson, will call you soon to arrange a time.

Sincerely,

Mark Davis

5.3　Business Letters

Written communication takes place between two or more parties. Business letters are written documents used for professional and work-related communication between businesses or between businesses and their customers, clients, or other entities, serving different purposes like business transactions, complaints, warnings, notices, invitations, declarations, information, apologies, and various other purposes. A business letter is a formal and professional way of correspondence in essence, and thus, is also known as an "official letter" "business correspondence letter" or "professional business letter". Business letters play a vital role in business. In dealing with business transactions, senders and receivers often use business letters for business inquiries, orders, circulars, claims, complaints, adjustment, and various other commercial reasons based on maintaining a good relationship with other companies or organizations.

A well-written business letter is an important communication medium, especially in a business transaction. It is used to help business people to communicate with customers, suppliers, debtors, creditors, public authorities, etc. to initiate, carry out, and conclude a transaction. For example, you can use the business letter to construct a relationship with business partners, to persuade your business partners to sign a contract with your company, to inform a potential client about the products of your company, to remind your business partner to follow up with the projects under cooperation, to reject a proposal or offer, to seek to obtain information, to call for action, to request financial support from your company for your project, to introduce troubleshooting strategies to your employer, to seek a position in a company, to introduce a person or policy, to formalize decisions, to express thanks, and many other purposes.

The world is getting more and more globalized and most of the business transactions are carried out through business correspondence. The expansion of the world market and quick transportation of goods have brought about a revolution in modern communication systems. Instead of sending managers and representatives to various customers or agencies for building business relationships and further interest in the business, the success of a modern business greatly depends on the use of business letters. A good business letter brings business people together, selling goods, bringing new clients, bringing back the lost customers, giving incentives to the dealers, building up confidence among the buyers, settling disputes, opening

Chapter **5** Basic Correspondence

new markets, and bringing more profits.

Businesses around the world take business letters very seriously and writing successful business letters helps you to be successful in your career. As you write a business letter, you will need to keep the following issues in mind:

- What should be included in a professional letter written for business purposes?
- How is a business letter structured with the essential components?
- How can you draft different kinds of business letters?
- What is your relationship with the reader?
- What is the cultural background of your reader?
- How can you revise and edit business letters?

Here is an example of work-related communication between the President's Office of ABC University in Canada and a professor from AAA University of Technology in China. The professor was invited to ABC University as a one-year visiting scholar, and was acting as a contactor between the two universities during the visit.

Regina, Saskatchewan

Canada S4S CA6

Phone: (220) 520–2020

Fax: (220) 520–1010

July 19, 2021

Ms. Susan Zhong

Department of English

AAA University of Technology

1111 South Gudong Road, Huli

Xiamen, Fujian, PRC 360000

Susanzhong@aaa.com

Dear Ms. Zhong,

I am pleased to extend this official invitation to you to join us at ABC University for one

---

115

(Continued)

year, beginning in September 2021 as an International Visiting Scholar in the Faculty of Arts, Department of International Languages. Dr. Larry Georgopolous will be your contact person on our campus. He can be reached at LarryGeorgopolous@uabc.edu.ca. We understand that you will be researching intercultural communication, lexicography, and English language teaching.

We understand that you will receive financial support from AAA University of Technology and will be responsible for your travel expenses, accommodation, food, books, and supplies. While here you will be provided access to the university library and other facilities.

You will need to present this letter of invitation to Citizenship and Immigration Canada (CIC) officials when you apply for your work permit and entry visa, which costs $150 (CAD). This permit will entitle you to free provincial health insurance coverage under the Saskatchewan Hospital Service Plan (SHSP), administered by Saskatchewan Health.

Please note that your appointment will be as a Visiting Research Scholar, which is not intended for individuals wishing to pursue an advanced degree. A request to transfer your status to that of a graduate student during the term of your appointment will not be permitted.

If you have any questions or concerns, do not hesitate to contact Dr. Georgopolous or Molly Aimes-Wothington in our Office of International Cooperation and Development (Molly. Aimes-Wothington@uabc.edu.ca). We would appreciate knowing when your visa is approved and what your flight schedule will be once it has been finalized, as we will arrange to have someone meet you at the airport. As well, please advise us regarding your housing preference. We're looking forward to meeting you in Regina.

Yours sincerely,

K. A. Priscilla

K. A. Priscilla, Ph.D.
Acting Vice-president (Research and International)
The President's Office
ABC University

Chapter 5 Basic Correspondence

5.3.1 Sections of Business Letters

As you can see from the above example, a business letter is a formal document with a set structure. A typical business letter usually consists of the following parts: the sender's address, the date, the inside address, the salutation, the main message, the complimentary close, and the signature. Let's make a closer study of each of these sections in a business letter one by one.

The Sender's Address

The sender's address (or return address) indicates who wrote the letter. Professional businesses usually have pre-designed the letterhead accompanied by a logo of the organization, showcasing the repute of the business. You can add something before the date like your address, phone number, fax number, website address, or email address in separate lines if the contact information is not provided on the letterhead. Skip a line between the address and the date.

The following is an example of the sender's address:

3035 Green Meadow Road
Regina, Saskatchewan
Canada S4S OA2

The following is another example of the sender's address:

1314 West Island Ring Road
Zhuhai, Guangdong Province
China 519000
Phone: 0756–2086698
Email: infozhuhai@163.com

The Date

The date is an important part of a business letter and is used for reference, indicating the date when the letter was written. Usually, the date is written in full with the day, month, and year, and included exactly below the letterhead or the sender's address with a separate line. Different countries may have different standards for formatting the date. In the United States, the date line puts the month first, and then includes the day and the year, for example "January

18, 2022". In Europe, the format for writing the date is the day, the month, and the year, for example "18 January, 2022".

The Inside Address

The inside address is the address of the recipient and contains the name, the title (if there is any), the company name, the street address, the city, the state/province, and the zip code / postal code of the recipient. It is professional to try to address a business letter to a specific individual instead of "President" "Manager" "Managing Director", etc. If you know the recipient, you can include title names like "Ms." "Mrs." "Mr.", and "Dr.". If you are not sure of the recipient and the title, try to make some research to identify the appropriate recipient. The phone number and email address can be added if necessary.

The following is the template:

Recipient's Name
Recipient's Title
Recipient's Company Name
Recipient's Street Address
Recipient's City, State/Province, Zip/Postal Code
Recipient's Phone Number: XXXX–XXXXXXX
Recipient's Email Address: recipient's name@website.com

The following is an example based on the above template of the inside address:

Mr. Steven Edwards
Sales Manager
ABC Office Supplies
1234 Sunrise Rd.
Buffalo, NY 2222–6666
Phone: 1234–2226666
Email: infoabc@yahoo.com

The Salutation

A formal business letter begins with a salutation like "Dear", followed by the title and the recipient's last name, showing respect to the recipient and usually ends with a comma or colon, for example "Dear Mr. Zhen,". Try to avoid the sexist "Dear Sir" "Gentlemen" or "Dear Madam" and the stilted "Ladies and Gentlemen" or "Dear Sir/Madam". Be sure to include the title of the recipient if you know it (such as "Ms." "Mrs." "Mr." or "Dr."). However, if you know the name of the recipient but you are not sure about the title or gender of the recipient, then use the full name, for example "Dr. Isaac Jones" " Mr. Eric Zhong". The salutation addressing a company or organization like "Dear Construction Bank" or "Dear Sales Team" can be used if you can't find out the specific individual recipient. Remember to check if you have used the same name included in the inside address for the salutation before sending the letter.

The Main Message

The main message is the most important part of a business letter. And the main message of a standard business letter usually consists of an introduction, a body and a conclusion. An introduction explains the subject, the purpose of the letter, the importance of the letter, any relevant background information, or the main point needed to be clarified. The body follows the introduction and can be one or more paragraphs, elaborating and providing more specific details. The last section is a conclusion, reiterating why you write, wrapping up and summarizing, or calling for action, also expressing thanks to the recipient.

The following is a sample inquiry letter sent to a commercial real estate agency inquiring about the availability of office space for lease. The main message of the inquiry letter has an introduction which states the writing purpose, a body which has one paragraph only, offering specific details, and a conclusion which is a call for action.

Dear Mr. Montoya,

We are inquiring about leasing commercial office space in the Xiamen International Convention and Exhibition Center which is located along the Island Ring Road.

Our company is an international exhibition company, and we seek a ground-floor location that is clearly visible from the Island Ring Road, with easy walk-in access as well as adequate parking adjacent to the office. We would be interested in leasing a space for 5 years on a month-to-month basis, and would like to be able to move in by October 16, 2022.

If you have any listings that would be suitable, please have an agent contact me as soon as possible to discuss.

Thank you for your consideration. I'm looking forward to hearing from you.

Sincerely,
Susan Cai
Susan Cai

The following is a complaint letter. The main message of the complaint letter introduces the customer, describes the problem and offers the resolution for the problem.

Dear Mr. Howard,

My name is Jason Trigg and I am writing to express my dissatisfaction with the computer I purchased on your official website on March 12, 2022.

It is not working effectively. Sometimes, it even breaks down in the process of running and can't start up. To resolve the issue, I request that a new computer be sent free of charge in place of the defective one I returned. If you are unable to send me a new one, I would like you to refund the full amount that I paid to my bank account.

Thank you for processing my claim within this week.

Sincerely yours,
Jason Trigg
Jason Trigg

The following is a sales letter for a travel agency to promote the travel services to an important client. The main message of the sales letter contains complete and well-drafted information. It has an introduction, stating the purpose of promoting the travel-related business, a body which offers specific details about the services, and a conclusion calling for action.

Chapter 5 Basic Correspondence

> Dear Mr. Jacob,
>
> The purpose of this letter is to introduce the travel-related services offered by our travel agency, ABC Travel Agency. We are a reputed travel agency offering a wide range of travel-related services for the last 10 years in the industry. All our services aim to meet all kinds of travel needs of our clients that range from tickets to accommodation reservations.
>
> Please find the brochure of all our services enclosed with the letter which also contains complete information on the travel packages offered by us and their prices for domestic and international traveling. We also specialize in custom-made travel packages that are designed as per your needs and desires at very competitive rates. Our services also include delivery of tickets at your doorstep without any extra payment.
>
> All you are required to do is to get in touch with our travel executive for all your travel needs and they will do all the planning in the shortest time for the most reasonable price. Feel free to contact us via the mail or telephone and we will be happy to attend to your queries. Please find all our contact details mentioned on our brochure.
>
> We hope to serve you with our travel services soon.
>
> Sincerely yours,
> *Andrew Mars*
> Andrew Mars
> CEO, ABC Travel Agency

The following is another example for further understanding. It is a confirmation letter sent from the hostel to the guest. The main message of the letter includes an introduction, stating the purpose of confirming reservation for the recipient, a body which offers specific details about the check-in and check-out services, room services, payment and other important information, and a conclusion which extends a warm welcome to the recipient.

The main message of this letter contains comprehensive and well-drafted information, and it helps to keep the guest well-informed of the room services, and develop a good relationship with the guest.

Dear David Lee,

We are pleased to confirm your reservation. Your account number is 223355. Please review the following information:

Arrival Date: February 18, 2022

Departure Date: February 24, 2022

Number of Nights: 6

Number of Persons: 1

Room Type Requested: Single room

Room Rate per Night: $175

If you would like to update the above information, please inform the residence services desk at: accomservice@residence.com.

—Guest information—
Check-in time is anytime after 4:00 p.m.
Check-out is anytime before 11:00 a.m.
Please inform us if you plan to arrive after midnight on your arrival date.

Please advise us no later than 4:00 p.m. on the day preceding your scheduled arrival so as to avoid overcharges. If you don't cancel before 4:00 p.m., your credit card will be charged for one night's stay.

Please note that all buildings are smoke-free. Guests who wish to smoke may do so 9 meters away from the building. We appreciate your understanding and compliance with this policy. Guests who require internet access can be set up by request upon check-in. We will provide linens, towels and pillows. Guests will need to supply their own personal hygiene items, such as soap, shampoo, etc. Parking is available for guests and visitors. The rates for daily, weekly and above ground parking can also be found.

—The Residence Services Desk is open 24 hours a day—
Breakfast: 7:30 a.m.–10:30 a.m.
Brunch on weekends/holidays: 10:00 a.m.–2:30 p.m.

For your convenience, we accept the following methods of payment: Visa, MasterCard,

> (Continued)
>
> CDN Money Orders, and CDN Currency. Please check-in at the Residence Services Desk. If you have any questions, please contact us. For more information regarding our accommodations, please visit our website.
>
> We're looking forward to seeing you.
>
> Sincerely,
> *Matthew Brown*
> Matthew Brown

The Complimentary Close

The complimentary close is a short and polite remark that ends your letter. The close begins one line after the last body paragraph. Capitalize the first word of your closing and leave four lines for a signature between the close and the sender's name. A comma should follow the closing which refers to the end of the letter. It is courteous and shows a mark of respect towards the recipient. "Yours sincerely" "Sincerely" "Yours respectfully" "Yours" "Best regards", etc. are usually used.

The Signature

A business letter is regarded as complete and legal when signed by the writer. Handwriting a signature adds a personal tone to the letter and shows professionalism. In a printed letter, the signature includes a handwritten signature as well as the printed full name. The signature is to write in black or blue ink. However, when the business letter is to be sent online, then the writer can use an electronic signature or the scanned image of the handwritten signature if it complies with the rules of the company or organization. When the writer is writing for a business or organization, the title should also be included immediately below the typed name.

5.3.2 Formats for Business Letters

Formats of business letters are verified. There are three kinds of basic formats used in business letters: full block formats, modified block formats, and semi-block formats. Any of these three kinds of basic formats are acceptable in a business letter.

Full Block Formats

The most common format of a professional business letter is known as the full block format and is also called the block format. It is the easiest format to use and the simplest to set up in the word processing program. In a full block business letter, all the text is aligned to the left margin. The entire letter from the beginning to the end, including the sender's address, the date, the recipient's address, the salutation, the main message, the complimentary close and the signature, is all left-justified. This type of format gives a clean and professional look to the letter.

The following is an example of a full block format:

---

162 Newton Avenue
San Diego, CA 92113–1005

April 12, 2022

Dr. Andrew Randall
Director of Education Programs
Constitution College
75 Green Mountain Street
Concord, CA 94519–1012

Dear Dr. Randall,

I would like to thank you for your recent letter confirming your interest in developing a mutually beneficial relationship between our two institutions. My appreciation goes out as well to President Johnson for his letter dated April 5, 2021, in which he graciously accepted our invitation to participate with us as a distinguished research partner.

As I indicated in my letter to President Johnson, our institution is currently embarking on an ambitious plan to strengthen its degree programs and expand its research activities to become one of the top academic and research institutions in the world. Central to that program's success is our quest to develop joint research initiatives in various scientific fields with selected premier world institutions, such as yours. We are therefore honored

Chapter 5 Basic Correspondence

(Continued)

> that we will be able to work as colleagues with your institution's distinguished leaders and outstanding faculty members to realize the objectives of our ambitious strategic plan.
>
> Following the receipt of President Johnson's letter of interest, I requested the appropriate departments here to develop a draft proposed framework agreement that would identify the areas of interest that our cooperation might encompass. Once such areas of common interest are agreed upon by both parties, I would look forward to welcoming you and other officers of your institution to formally sign the Cooperation Agreement shortly.
>
> Accordingly, with your permission, I have taken the liberty of drafting the enclosed sample agreement for your review. You will notice that the draft Cooperation Agreement is titled "service contract" agreement. That is the standard terminology that we use for all of our cooperation agreements with distinguished institutions. Such a title is necessary to meet various administrative and legal requirements that govern our budgetary process. I hope that the proposed areas of cooperation that we have put forward are acceptable to you. I'm looking forward to receiving your views and comments soon.
>
> Thank you again for your support and cooperation.
>
> Sincerely,
> *Jeffrey Hutchinson*
> Jeffrey Hutchinson
> Director, Education Programs
> Bradley Institution for Science

Modified Block Formats

Another commonly used letter format is known as the modified block format which is a convenient way of writing formal business letters. Modified block business letters use a slightly different format from the full block business letters. In the modified block style, the sender's address, date, complimentary close and the signature line are slightly to the right of the center of the paper. Paragraphs of the modified block letter format are usually not indented and are aligned to the left margin of the page.

The following is a business letter example in the modified block format:

>   1321 North Western Drive
>   Toronto, ON, M3F 2N1
>   312–222–1115
>   Ericlee@email.com
>
>   March 16, 2022
>
> Laurie Wang
> Head of Operations
> DCP Technological Services
> 1256 Broadway Drive
> Toronto, ON, S2R S9P
> 623–999–3366
>
> Dear Mr. Wang,
>
> I am writing to inquire about the support of your technological products, specifically your budgeting, system management, and data analysis software.
>
> Oriental Financial Service is a top financial firm located in Toronto which specializes in providing clients with the most effective financial advice. We work with a wide range of multinational companies, including Seagull Enterprises, Global Logistics Company, Broadway Broadcasting Cooperation, and Tango Travel Agency. To optimize our services, we're keen on upgrading our system to offer better services to our customers at home and abroad. An updated management system embedded with efficient data analysis and effective budgeting software is top on our purchasing list. We want to receive a cost estimate for incorporating your technological products into our management system.
>
> You can reach out to me through any of my contact details above. We're looking forward to your reply and anticipate a positive working relationship and a good cooperation with your company.
>
>   Yours sincerely,

Chapter 5 Basic Correspondence

(Continued)

> *Eric Lee*
> Eric Lee
> Head of Operations
> Oriental Financial Service

Semi-block Formats

The semi-block format resembles the modified block format in every other regard except that the paragraphs are indented. The following is an example for a business letter using the semi-block format:

> 1321 North Western Drive
> Toronto, ON, M3F 2N1
> 312–222–1115
> Ericlee@email.com
>
> April 21, 2022
>
> Laurie Wang
> Head of Operations
> DCP Technological Services
> 1256 Broadway Drive
> Toronto, ON, S2R S9P
> 623–999–3366
>
> Dear Mr. Wang,
>
>   We are happy to inform you that during the board of directors meeting held on April 19, 2022, your proposal for the provision of your technological products and services to our company in the forthcoming financial year was chosen. Everyone was satisfied with the details mentioned in the proposal. We would like to offer you the contract for one year.
>
>   We will be sending a representative from our company to you to sign the contract and to complete the paperwork for our future cooperation. As you had mentioned, we decided

(Continued)

> to stick to the price specified in your proposal. The entire amount will be paid in three installments. The first installment will be given on the contract date, and the remaining two within two months at separate times.
>
> We shall rely on your services as your company is well-known for its quality services. We're looking forward to having a cordial relationship with your company.
>
> Yours sincerely,
> *Eric Lee*
> Eric Lee
> Head of Operations
> Oriental Financial Service

5.4 Memos

The memorandum is one of the most common forms of business communication which transmits information between colleagues or departments within a company or an organization. According to *Oxford Advanced Learner's Dictionary*, a memorandum is an official note from one person to another in the same organization, a proposal or report on a particular subject for a person, an organization, a committee, etc. The word "memo" is a colloquial form of "memorandum"; the plural of "memo" is "memos", while the plural of "memorandum" is "memoranda" or "memorandums".

Internal communication and external communication are two main types of written communication systems that exist in the business area. The memorandum is mostly used for internal communication. Before email was widely used as a form of business communication, the interoffice memorandum played a vital role in internal communication. Memos are highly efficient because they convey the writers' ideas quickly and directly to the readers. And as memos go between co-workers and colleagues, they play an important part in keeping different parts of a company or an organization in touch.

As you write memos, you will need to keep the following issues in mind:

- What is the function of a memo?
- How is a memo structured?
- How many types of memos are there?
- What should be emphasized in a memo to achieve successful communication?

The following is an example of a memorandum issued by Sunshine University of Technology on travel vouchers for faculty and staff members:

MEMORANDUM

To: SUT Faculty & Staff Members
From: Melissa Johnson, Chief Financial Officer
Date: April 9, 2022
Subject: Travel Vouchers

We would like to make it easier for you to get reimbursed for your expenses when you travel on business and get your payment back in a timely manner. The following are some rules concerning travel vouchers:

- Travel vouchers must be submitted to the Financial Management Center within seven days of returning from a business trip.
- Receipts are required for transportation, lodging, taxis, and all other business-related expenses.
- Receipts should clearly indicate the vendor, date, itemized purchases, and a total amount spent.
- If required receipts are not available, a statement, signed by the traveler, certifying the amount paid will be accepted.
- Lodging reimbursement requests must be accompanied by an itemized receipt.
- If you share a room with someone, ask the hotel to split the billing between the two parties so you have a receipt for your part of the room bill only.
- Receipts are also required for baggage storage and handling, car rentals, and other fees.

When to Use a Travel Voucher
- To reimburse faculty or staff members for business travel expenses.

(Continued)

- Travel expenses for non-employees must be reimbursed by invoice-voucher.
- The name of the conference, the date, and the place the conference was held should be provided.
- The traveler's name, job title, ID number, address, and bank account should be provided.
- Provide detailed information about transportation tools, departure and destination (including the city and province), dates and times of arrival and departure.

Non-reimbursable Expenses

- Alcoholic beverages
- Entertainment
- Late check-out and room guarantee charges

The following is another example of a memorandum issued by a university to all faculty and staff members:

MEMORANDUM

To: All Faculty and Staff
From: Ronnie Wright, Chancellor
Date: August 26, 2021
Subject: Formation of Wellness Policy Team

I'm very pleased to announce the formation of Wellness Policy Team, chaired by Steve Holland, Vice Chancellor of our university. The team is charged with leading the implementation of the wellness policy, which addresses the nutrition education, physical activity and all kinds of food services available on campus. The team will be recommending ways to provide nutritious yet tasty food options so that students and staff can choose healthier foods for their meals and snacks. We are also looking at ways to increase opportunities for physical activity. Studies have demonstrated that a program of regular physical activity results in a reduction in disruptive behaviors in the classroom and an increase in students' time on task.

(Continued)

> Wellness is a team effort involving everyone in our university community. You will be encouraged to support and get involved in the implementation activities of our wellness policy. Studies show a direct connection between the health status and academic achievement. Our wellness policy is a very positive and exciting step for our university. By improving the health environment and practices, we will be improving our health and academic achievement.
>
> The team meets monthly and you are invited to attend. The next meeting will be held at 3 p.m. next Tuesday at Student Center.
>
> We will have regular reports from the Wellness Policy Team at staff meetings. If you have any questions, please feel free to contact me.

5.4.1 Functions of Memorandums

Memorandums are used for different purposes in the organization, to inform, to persuade, to identify a problem, to propose a solution, or to provide or request factual information. In large companies or organizations, people often use memorandums and other means of internal communication to communicate with branches, offices, and colleagues when dealing with different work-related matters. Memorandums are intended to be read and acted upon by executives, branch managers, supervisors, or staff members. The detailed function of memorandums is discussed below from different perspectives.

Memorandums are used to provide a response to requests and sometimes to be used when the superior requests someone to perform a particular job. It is very useful for proving suggestions and instructions to the subordinates. Managers and supervisors use it to give necessary suggestions and invaluable instructions so that the subordinates can perform the activities properly. The memorandum is used to make any request to different parties in the organization. It is frequently used by the managers and subordinates requesting others for attending any meeting, executing any action, soliciting favor, or for some other purposes.

Memorandums are widely used to convey information on different affairs to the people working in the organization. New policies, changes to existing policies, decisions, appointments of managers, clarifications, announcements, etc. are communicated in the form of memorandums. Some mishaps or misunderstandings between persons may occur within an organization and office memorandums can be used to seek an explanation from a certain person on particular issues so that corrective measures may be taken.

Memorandums can be used for providing solutions to particular problems. Sometimes, managers and supervisors issue memorandums to provide necessary instructions to the subordinates for better performance of the daily activities. Sometimes, memorandums are used to present informal reports to the superiors. Informal reports presented in memorandum form are usually short and informational. Findings and recommendations are presented by such a memorandum which helps managers to take proper decisions.

All in all, a memorandum performs different functions to carry out the purpose for which it is used. Due to the communication and reference value, memorandums are often used in different companies and organizations and are usually carefully indexed, filed, and preserved, facilitating ready sourcing and reference.

5.4.2　General Discussion on the Format of Memorandums

A memorandum indicates who sends it and who the intended recipients are. The date and subject lines are also presented, followed by a message that contains an opening, a summary with discussion, and a conclusion. Each part has a clear purpose. The following is a template of a memorandum in formal style:

MEMORANDUM

To: [Recipient]

From: [Person and/or Department issuing the memorandum]

CC: [Send copies to anyone who needs to know the information, but no action is expected. However, not all memorandums have "CC" recipients. "CC" recipients can also be listed after the Conclusion.]

Date: [Date sent]

Subject: [Subject of the memorandum]

[Opening—Get to the point in the opening paragraph. Keep things simple and short. Make it easy to read.]

(Continued)

> [Summary and Discussion—Summarize any historical or contextual information needed to support the opening paragraph and discuss with detailed and specific information.]
>
> [Conclusion—End with a call to action.]
>
> Attachments: [List any attachments to the memorandum. However, not all memorandums have attachments and only items referred to in the body of the memorandum are to be listed.]

5.4.3 Detailed Discussion on the Format of Memorandums

Memorandums are often divided into the following sections to organize information: the heading, the opening section, the summary and discussion section, the closing section, and the attachment when necessary. Let's make a closer study of each of these sections.

The Heading

The first part of a memorandum is the heading segment which gives information about the writer, the intended recipient, the date, and sometimes the names of other people who may see the memorandum and the subject. Some companies and organizations design, purchase, or print their memorandum stationery with the heading to save the writer some time when he or she is preparing memorandums. Thus, the format of memorandums varies from company to company, from organization to organization. However, all memorandums, regardless of formats, include the following parts: the writer, the recipient, the date, and the subject in the heading segment and there is not a set order for the parts of the heading.

The following is a general format for writing a heading:

> **MEMORANDUM**
>
> **To:** Name and job title of the recipient of the message
> **From:** Name and job title of the writer of the message
> **Date:** Complete date when the memorandum was sent
> **Subject (or RE):** What the memorandum is about

Although a memorandum is interoffice business communication, the recipient should be addressed formally and appropriately. A full name and title of the writer and the recipient should be used. The complete date should be included with the month, the date, and the year. Write "January 10, 2022" or "10 January, 2022". The subject line should be concise, specific, and to the point, giving the reader an idea of what the memorandum is about.

The following is an example for writing a heading:

MEMORANDUM

To: Edward Jones, Sales Manager
From: Mary Lee, Secretary
Date: January 12, 2021
Subject (or RE): Market Meeting

If you are sending a memorandum to the entire staff, you might write "To: All Employees". For example:

MEMORANDUM

To: All Employees
From: Mary Lee, Secretary
Date: January 12, 2021
Subject (or RE): Market Meeting

The "CC" line indicates who will receive a "Courtesy Copy" of the memorandum. This is not the person to whom the memorandum is directed. Rather, this is someone who may need to stay informed about policies or issues that you're addressing in the memorandum. For example:

MEMORANDUM

To: Edward Jones, Sales Manager
From: Mary Lee, Secretary
CC: Susan Durst, Human Resources Manager
Date: January 12, 2021
Subject (or RE): Market Meeting

The heading should be at the top of the page, aligned to the left-hand side of the page. Usually, "memorandum" is capitalized and typed at the top of the page to show that this document is a memorandum at the outset. The first letters of "To" "From" "Date", and "Subject" are usually capitalized.

The Opening

The gist of a memorandum should occur in the opening segment which is usually an introductory paragraph or sentences stating briefly and explicitly the purpose and subject of the memorandum, the context and problem, and a preview of the specific assignment or task. Including the purpose of the memorandum at the opening part will help to clarify the reason for the recipient to read it and to forecast what is in the rest of the memorandum. A paragraph or a few sentences can be used to establish the background and state the problem to be solved.

The Summary and Discussion Section

This section summarizes any historical or contextual information needed to support the opening paragraph and discusses it with detailed and specific information.

The summary helps the reader to understand the key points of the memorandum immediately. The discussion is the longest part of the memorandum, in which supporting details are included, starting with the most general information and moving to specific or supporting ideas, facts, and research that back up the argument in the memorandum. Strong and adequate points and evidence should be included to persuade the reader to follow the recommended actions. Lists, instead of paragraphs, with sentences can also be used for presenting important points or details. The lists should be parallel in grammatical form.

The Closing

Close the memorandum with a courteous ending stating the actions suggested for the reader to take, considering how the reader will benefit from the desired actions and how to make the actions easier. Sentences like "I will be glad to discuss this recommendation with you during our Tuesday trip to the spa and follow through on any decisions you make." "If there are questions about any topics listed, please contact Lisa Lee at 520–214–2021." "For questions regarding this memorandum, please contact Wayne Carlton (052) 921–2901 or Greg Moseley (052) 921–2920." can be used at the closing segment.

The Attachment (If Necessary)

Make sure you document your findings or provide detailed information whenever necessary. You can do this by attaching lists, graphs, tables, etc. at the end of your memorandum. Be sure to refer to your attachments in your memorandum and add a notation about what is attached below your closing.

The following is an example of the main message of a memorandum structured with the opening, summary, discussion, and closing section:

Opening Section

There are five Early Middle College (EMC) policy changes and updates. Please share this with EMCs operating within your school district(s).

Summary and Discussion Section

Policy on EMC Grade Progression Reporting

Students have a fifth year to fulfill diploma and degree/certificate requirements. The fifth year requires one grade level to be reported for two consecutive school years. Beginning with the 2020–2021 school year, Grade 12 is the only grade level expected to be reported twice in consecutive school years. This means that the sequence of grade levels reported for an EMC student, over their high school and fifth year, is expected to be 9, 10, 11, 12. This requirement is also included in the most recent EMC FAQ document.

Updated EMC FAQs

The EMC FAQ document has been updated and can be found at the following link. This version supersedes all previous versions. https://www.michigan.gov/123456...html.

2019–2020 Pupil Accounting Manual

EMC sections of the Pupil Accounting Manual (PAM) have been updated. Please review the PAM for EMC on-track graduation requirements and documents needed for a successful pupil accounting audit. The PAM can be found here: https://www.michigan.gov/654321...html.

Coding Appeals Process

An EMC Coding Appeals Process has been developed. Districts may appeal to late code students who were not properly coded by the fall certification of 2019. You can find the appeal process and forms on the MDE website: https://www.michigan.gov/123456...html. Important note: This appeal process does not affect Section 61b funding eligibility for Career

(Continued)

and Technical Education EMC students that were incorrectly coded during the appealed year—regardless of the appeal outcome.

Updated EMC Application Assurances

For school districts applying to open a new EMC in 2020, the application is due February 3, 2020, and the assurances section of the application has been revised. The updated application may be found at the following link: https://www.michigan.gov/123456...html. The application must include signatures on the updated assurances and signature page. For EMC students meeting Goal 1 and Goal 4 listed in Michigan's Top 10 Strategic Education Plan: provide every child access to an aligned, high-quality P-20 system from early childhood to post-secondary attainment—through a multi-stakeholder collaboration with business and industry, labor, and higher education—to maximize lifetime learning and success. Goal 4: reduce the impact of high-risk factors, including poverty, and provide equitable resources to meet the needs of all students to ensure that they have access to quality educational opportunities.

Closing Section

If there are questions about any topics listed, please contact Lisa Seigel at 517–241–2072 or seigel@michigan.gov.

5.4.4 Types of Memorandums

Memorandums are used in a variety of communication situations in the workplace, from documentation of procedures and policies to simple announcements, serving the function of notifying events that occurred, conveying decisions, meeting agendas, policies, internal reports, and short proposals, giving instructions, offering ideas and suggestions, confirming procedures, seeking information and a variety of events relating to the workplace. The following are some common types of memorandums classified according to their basic functions.

Instruction Memorandums

An instruction memorandum could be something as simple as using the photocopier machine, or something more complex, such as a code of conduct in the office. It is a mini how-to guide that gives the recipients basic directions on how to do something. It could be the summary of some major procedures that have just been implemented or some rules or guidelines about after-hours security, or about a change in policy or the like of something happens. In the workplace, an instruction memorandum is useful for the management to provide clear and concise instructions or directions for the employees to follow.

Suggestion Memorandums

Recipients are requested to give their opinions on certain issues and specify how they should put forward the suggestions. A suggestion memorandum is written when the management is requesting views from the employees or asks subordinates for suggestions for tackling certain problems.

Confirmation Memorandums

A confirmation memorandum is designed to restate the terms of the demand or agreement and encourage the recipients to ask for clarification for detailed information. It is written to confirm in writing certain demand or agreement that has been agreed to verbally.

Request Memorandums

A request memorandum is designed to gain a favorable response to a request in a convincing way, trying to win the heart of the recipients by using persuasive language and to get a favor from a certain person or group of people.

Proposal Memorandums

A proposal memorandum intends to convey a plan of action or simply a proposal to the recipients and it highlights the key points to a certain plan or proposal and provides steps in the execution of the plan or the proposal.

Report Memorandums

A report memorandum is written after a certain period to give an account of the progress, for example trip reports, cost control reports, sales reports which are to be submitted at regular intervals. Since report memorandums are written frequently, they are often designed and preprinted for enhancing the efficiency of writing.

Announcement Memorandums

Announcement memorandums can be written to give positive and negative news to employees throughout a company or an organization for information relating to positive news like promotion opportunities and job openings, or negative news like cut back announcements.

The following are examples for further understanding of different types of memorandums. The first example is an instruction memorandum focusing on the directions and tasks that the writer wants to instruct the recipient.

MEMORANDUM

To: Bill Erp, Sales Manager
From: Russ Hamilton, Executive Secretary
Date: September 29, 2019
Subject: Bidding Plan for Better Widget Makers Bakery Contract

Better Widget Makers has asked us to submit an annual cost estimate for supplying bakery products to their new cafeteria. Their purchasing officer needs our information by the 10th of October to present it to her finance committee by the 20th. She has requested the following information:
- Wholesale price sheets
- Quantity cost breakdowns
- Annual contract discounts
- Delivery and other service charges.

Specifically, they are interested in regular deliveries of fresh pastries, pies, dinner rolls, and sandwich bread. They have 1,500 employees working full time, so in our proposal, we need to make some practical suggestions that will help them to decide how many items they will need to order, and how often.

Bill, I need your help putting together a comprehensive information packet describing the individual items in our product line. Please meet with Rachel in the Pastry Department and John in the Bread Department for their input. They both have experience preparing large bids and will know just what products and quantities to suggest.

You and I can then get together with Annie in Accounting to run the numbers. I'll schedule some time with her on Monday, October 6, and let you know when that meeting will occur.

> Thanks, Bill. I know this is a short notice, but it's a great opportunity to take on a major new customer. With all of us pulling together, I am confident we can land this account.
>
> CC: Rachel Cohen, Supervisor, Pastry Department
>   John Silvers, Supervisor, Bread Department

The second example is a request memorandum used to communicate with employees when the management needs to make requests for internal business affairs.

> **MEMORANDUM**
>
> **To:** All Directors Responsible for Submission of Budgets
> **From:** James Hamilton, Manager, Finance Department
> **Date:** November 1, 2019
> **Subject:** 2020 Budget to Be Submitted
>
> You are hereby notified to submit on or before November 20, 2019, the budget of your office for the fiscal year 2020. Please refer to the enclosed Fiscal Year 2020 Budget of the Company for the related procedures, guidelines, and principles.
>
> The Fiscal Year 2020 Budget of the Company is provided for the preparation and submission of budget estimates. Please submit the budget of your office to Finance Department with detailed plans. Any question regarding the procedures, guidelines, and principles should be directed to Finance Department.
>
> Your cooperation in submitting the Budget in time before the deadline will be appreciated by all concerned.

Besides being classified according to the functions, memorandums can also be classified according to the way of circulation, such as memorandums to upper management (which flow upward from the individual employees to the management), memorandums to lower employees (which flow down from the management to the individual employees), memorandums to divisions affiliated, memorandums to all staff, and memorandums to colleagues in and outside the department.

5.5 Emails

The email is widely used as a form of highly effective business communication tool in the workplace and it has become a way of working in the workplace. We read and compose emails almost every day. Using emails in business can increase work efficiency and productivity since emails reach their recipients instantly through the internet and the messages will be stored until the recipients are ready to read. Furthermore, we can quickly and easily send electronic files, such as text documents, photos, and data sheets to several contacts or a large number of recipients simultaneously by attaching them to an email.

The email is a very convenient way for communication both in and outside a company or an organization. It can be delivered and circulated inside a company or an organization, serving major purposes like sharing information, coordinating actions, and satisfying social needs. More and more businesses are capitalizing on emails for networking business and trade, establishing business relations, getting customers, marketing goods and services, dealing with business concerning inquiries and replies, offers and counteroffers, orders and contracts, payments, packing and shipment, insurance, complaints and claims, etc.

As you write emails, you will need to keep in mind the following issues:

- What are the functions of emails in the workplace?
- What should be emphasized in the email for achieving a successful communication target?
- How is an email structured?

The following is a case of capitalizing on emails to establish the relationship between two universities, ABC University in Canada and AAA University in China. In this case, Jack Goodman is a lecturer at ABC University and also the Head of International Business Development. Jasmine Lee is a professor and director of the English Department, Faculty of International Languages, AAA University. The two universities are seeking cooperation opportunities for recruiting and supporting students for international programs.

The following two emails are based on the first contact between Jasmine Lee and Jack Goodman, the representatives of the two universities. The two emails help to establish the relationship between the two universities.

The current email system can automatically add the sender's details, including full name, professional title, address, etc., at the end of the email.

Dear Jack,

Thank you for your email and I am writing to welcome you to AAA University. I am Jasmine Lee, Director of English Department, Faculty of International Languages of AAA University.

The International Office of my university forwarded me your last email seeking possible cooperation between the two universities. And I was informed that April 19 and April 23 are the possible dates of your arrival and you are going to give a lecture to our students.

We are presently checking with students for the possible time of the lecture and will confirm the date of giving the lecture before tomorrow morning. It is my great honor to get to know you in virtual space and I'm looking forward to seeing you soon in person in AAA University.

Best regards,

Jasmine

Jasmine Lee
Professor
Director of English Department
Faculty of International Languages
AAA University
Siming, Xiamen, Fujian
PRC 350002

Dear Jasmine,

Thank you very much for your efficient response in organizing a suitable time for me to come and visit AAA University to speak with your students. I feel the time you suggest would be suitable for me. I expect that my talk will last approximately 45 minutes and then I will allow plenty of time afterward for questions and answers. Therefore 7:30–9:30 p.m.

(Continued)

on Friday should be suitable.

I have also copied my colleague Jessie Lian from the International Office into this email on the off chance she is available to join me for the talk.

Please provide me with the following information so that I can fully prepare for the talk, and organize my transportation and hotel accommodation:

- The address of your university in Pinyin and Chinese.
- The approximate number of students you envisage attending the talk. As there are approximately 180 students, the more the merrier. I would like to bring some materials to give to the students and therefore need to know roughly how many will attend.
- The year of study the attending students are currently in.
- The time and place to meet at AAA University.
- Finally, please can you provide a classroom with a computer and PPT facilities?

Thank you in advance for taking the time to coordinate my visit. It would be my honor to visit your institution and meet with your students.

I'm thoroughly looking forward to meeting with you soon and working with you closely in the future.

Kind regards,

Jack

Jack Goodman
Lecturer
Head of International Business Development
ABC University
Shanghai Institute of Foreign Trade Office
C215, 1900 Wenxiang Road

(Continued)

Songjiang, Shanghai
PRC 201620

E: JackGoodman@gmail.com
O: + 86(0)21 6710 3399

The following two emails are based on the contact between Jasmine Lee and Jack Goodman, confirming information for the visit of Jack Goodman to AAA University.

Dear Jack,

I am writing to confirm that you are coming to give a lecture to our students (150–180) on Friday night, April 26, so that we can arrange the lecture room and other necessary facilities and inform our students.

Please find attached an itinerary for your visit and lecture. We hope to see you in AAA University and we're looking forward to meeting you on April 25 at the airport.

Yours sincerely,

Jasmine

Dear Jasmine,

Thank you for your email. Yes, I can confirm that I will be giving the talk to students on Friday, April 26. I have booked my flight tickets and have booked a hotel. I will send one further email shortly, with the details of my hotel to organize a meeting with the International Office of AAA University to be picked up. Therefore, please go ahead and book the lecture room and inform the students.

My colleague Jessie Lian will also be joining me to offer support for the students and answer any questions the students may have in Chinese.

I hope you enjoy the rest of your weekend and I will be in touch again very soon with the

(Continued)

details of my hotel.

Thank you once again for your cooperation in organizing my visit and I am looking forward to meeting with you soon. I hope together with our combined efforts we can encourage some students to study at ABC University next September and further strengthen our cooperation.

Kind regards,

Jack

The following email is sent from Jack Goodman to Jasmine Lee, expressing appreciation for the successful visit and the hope for further cooperation between the two universities.

Dear Jasmine,

It was my pleasure to meet you both this Friday and an honor to visit your institution to speak with your polite and enthusiastic students. Thank you both very much for your hospitality and for taking the time to help organize my guest lecture. Furthermore, I am very grateful for your joining me to support the talk on your Friday evening. I understand how busy you must be these days. As requested, please find my PPT attached to this email for your future reference.

I thoroughly enjoyed giving the talk and hope that the students now know a little more about our articulation program and the benefits of coming to study at ABC University. As we discussed, it would certainly be a good idea for me to speak with your students again perhaps next semester in October to give them time to think, discuss, and ask any questions they may have. I am sure this is something that can be discussed nearer to the time.

I am hopeful that we can continue to strengthen our cooperation and I'm thoroughly looking forward to working with you in the future.

Kindest regards,

Jack

The following email is sent from Jack Goodman to Jasmine Lee, sharing information on the progress of the program.

> Dear Jasmine,
>
> As always it is very nice to hear from you. How is your semester going so far? I hope everybody at AAA University is well.
>
> I am very pleased to hear that some students plan to study at ABC University this coming September, that is fantastic news and hopefully can be the stepping stone to further developing our partnership.
>
> I was pleased to receive an email and a phone call from one of your students this morning, who seems very eager to study at ABC University this coming September. This is great and thank you very much for passing on my contact details. Please encourage any other students to contact me personally with any questions or Wendy Wen from the International Office (copied into this email) and both Wendy and I will be more than happy to answer any questions and offer pre-departure support for any interested students.
>
> If any teaching staff of AAA University would like to know more information about the programs so they can inform their students, please encourage them to contact me also as I would be more than happy to help.
>
> Thank you once again for getting in touch and I wish you a very peaceful weekend.
>
> Kind regards,
>
> Jack

This case showcases the power of emails in international communication. Emails provide an efficient and effective way to transmit all kinds of electronic data. Well-written, clear, and effective emails not only save our time and enhance productivity but also prove us to be professional.

5.5.1 General Discussion on the Format of Emails

Emails can be categorized as formal, semi-formal, and informal emails. Although there are different categories, the email writing format is likewise. However, depending upon different categories, the selection of language varies. Professional, precise, and formal language should be utilized in formal emails while friendly and casual writing is employed in informal emails.

In the workplace, informal, semi-formal, and formal emails are used daily for internal and external affairs. However, it's important to format emails professionally when using emails to deal with business-related matters, and the message should be formatted like a typical business letter. The following is a template of a formal email:

From: Sender's email address

To: Recipient's email address

CC: Other concerned recipients with a visible email address

BCC: Other concerned recipients with an invisible email address

Subject: Major subject or purpose of writing

Salutation: A greeting showing respect to the reader

Main Body: Elaboration on the purpose of the email specifically with detailed information. Several paragraphs can be written in a formal email for a detailed discussion of the message.

Closing: A friendly sign-off

Signature: Name and contact details

First Name + Last Name

Address

Phone

5.5.2 Detailed Discussion on the Format of Emails

The email is one of the most common forms of communication in the workplace.

An effective email depends a lot on your professionalism and your communication skills. Emails are often divided into the following sections to organize basic information: subject, salutation, main body, closing, and signature.

The Subject

The subject line summarizes the content of the email message briefly and clearly.

The Salutation

Different salutations should be chosen accordingly, depending on the nature of your relationship with the recipient. An appropriate greeting shows respect to the reader. A formal email salutation like "Dear Mr./Ms. Last Name" "Dear Sir or Madam", or "Dear Manager" should be used if you've never met the recipient, while a more casual salutation can be used if a friendly, personal relationship with the recipient has been constructed. Email salutations also set the tone for the email, depending on the purpose of writing. A formal email salutation should be used if you are dealing with a very professional business occasion. A less formal or casual salutation like "Dear Joe" is a good choice if you're sending a note to express thanks to your colleague for a birthday celebration held for you.

The Main Body

The body of an email should be written clearly and concisely with a specific purpose so that the recipient will incline to read it. Several paragraphs can be written in a formal email for a detailed discussion of the message that you want to deliver. The first paragraph should include the information on your writing purpose directly and clearly. For example, if you want to establish a relationship for business cooperation, state it in your opening sentences. The middle paragraph usually describes what type of cooperation you are seeking, what the prospect of the cooperation for both parties is, and what you can offer for the cooperation. The final paragraph is to conclude your mail by expressing your gratitude and your hope for future cooperation.

The Closing

An appropriate closing with polite and professional language leaves your reader with a positive impression and can be the motivating factor and a call to action. The following are some of the most popular sign-offs for formal emails: "All the best" "Best regards" "Kind regards" "Respectfully" "Respectfully yours" "Sincerely" "Sincerely yours" "Yours truly".

Chapter 5 Basic Correspondence

The Signature

A signature is a way of signing off for your email and will have an impact on the recipient. A professional email signature is a tool for marketing your company or yourself and may offer an opportunity for connection with your recipient. The signature of a professional email usually includes your name, job title, company name, and phone number. An address and your company's website can also be included.

The following is an example based on the format:

From: Scott Shannon@gmail.com
To: Carol Goodsman@126.com
CC: Jack Moser@hotmail.com
BCC: Joe Lee@gmail.com

Subject: Check-in Service

Dear Carol,

Please check-in at your convenience as our hotel is open 24 hours and there are 3 ways to get to our location from Pearson International Airport:

1) Taxi—this is an approximately $60.00 CAD flat rate (please be sure to request a flat rate from the driver or they will go by the meter rate which will be higher).

2) Toronto Public Transit (TTC)—$3.25 CAD cash fare—take the 192 airport rocket bus to Kipling Subway Station (this is the terminal station), then get on the subway where you will get off at St. George Station, transfer to the Southbound Subway line, and then get off at Museum Subway Station. From here you will exit and walk east about 1–2 minutes on Charles Street West. Our building address is 140 Charles Street West and is on the North Side behind the Goldring Student Center building located at 150 Charles Street West.

3) UP Express Train—$12.00—there is a train service from the Pearson Airport to Union Subway Station. You will transfer to the TTC (Subway) at Union Station on the University Line ($3.25) and then head to Museum Station. Exit Museum Subway Station and walk 1–2

(Continued)

minutes on Charles Street West. Our building address is 140 Charles Street West and is on the North Side behind the Goldring Student Center building located at 150 Charles Street West.

The rates I have provided are one way, per person.

We are looking forward to your arrival and hope to see you soon.

Kind regards,

Scott Shannon
Attendant, Residence Services
University of Toronto
140 Charles Street West
27 King's College Circle
Toronto, Ontario M5S 1A1 Canada

O: 416–978–2011

Chapter 5 Basic Correspondence

> **Exercises**

1. Following the AIDA model, write a persuasive email requesting your readers to purchase your product or service. Remember to show your readers something of their concerns, explain benefits and give facts that will enhance your appeal in the interest and desire sections, gain credibility for you and your request, convince your readers that purchasing your product or service will help them to solve a significant problem, and close with a request for specific action.

2. Write a good news letter to the customers to announce the opening of a new branch of outlets in the city downtown of Xiamen.

3. Write a business letter based on the full block style, following the offered guidance.

Sender's Address

Date

Recipient's Name
Recipient's Address

Dear Mr./Ms. Whomever,

In the first paragraph, introduce what you are writing about and what you want from him or her.

In the subsequent paragraphs, explain the nature of your problem and what he or she can do for you. Be straight to the point.

In the last paragraph, be sure to thank the recipient for his or her time and efforts on your behalf. Also, let him or her know that you will contact him or her or that he or she can contact you with any questions.

Sincerely yours,
(four spaces so that your signature may appear here)

Signature

151

4. **Suppose you work for the Sales Department of Sunshine Shopping Mall, and write an email to the clients with the subject line and the structure given.**

> **Subject Line:** A Discount Coupon for You
>
> Dear _____,
>
> Thank you so much for _____.
>
> It's because of the support of clients like you that we have been able to be in business for such a long time. To thank you for your support, _____
> _____
> _____
>
> Please see the attachment for electronic coupons. _____
> _____
>
> The offer is only available for _____
> _____
>
> Yours sincerely,
>
> (Your signature)

Chapter 6
Reports

Reports are common features for most businesses and professions. Reports provide accounts of information and range from short, informal emails to over 100-page formal manuscripts. They may be distributed to internal or external readers, read via hard copy or on a computer screen, and written in a variety of business genres. Reports, like all professional communication, must be well written: clear, comprehensive, and well-organized. In addition, reports must be meticulously cited to give them credit because they often contain information obtained from a wide variety of sources.

This chapter provides an overview of the most common types of reports, the procedures of creating reports and the various formats used to present reports. It also provides you with techniques to effectively develop reports.

In this chapter, you will learn about:

- report types;
- report components;
- procedures of creating reports;
- meeting minutes and agendas;
- executive summaries;
- proposal reports;
- surveys.

6.1 Report Types

Some people divide reports into informal reports and formal reports. Whether a report is informal or formal depends on the readers and writing purposes. Informal reports are usually short—often two to three pages, although they can be much longer—and they are often internal to an organization. Short reports require that you write for readers who need particular information to complete their work successfully. Your organization will require you to write informal reports at some point in your career. You may need to report on the status of a working project, respond to questions, report on a trip that you've taken, summarize test activities, or describe an incident. At some point in your professional or business career, you may be called upon to write a formal report, either on your own or as part of a team. The project could be a business proposal, a company annual report, or an in-depth problem-solving study that answers questions (e.g. Should our company invest in the natural gas industry at this time?). It could also be a report of a scientific experiment or an inquiry or a technical document.

No matter whether the reports are long or short, formal or informal, typical reports fall into two major types—informative reports and analytical reports.

Informative reports, as the name implies, give information. An informative report can be periodic, such as an annual report that presents an organization's financial and administrative situation for the past year or fiscal year, or a progress report on how well a particular task is proceeding. An academic essay can be an informative report if it gives in-depth information about a particular topic. However, informative reports typically don't make recommendations; they just present the facts.

Analytical reports interpret data or information and often provide recommendations. They may be written to assess a business opportunity, provide solutions to problems, or support business decisions. Analytical reports analyze problems or issues and can take many forms, but among the most common are problem-solving reports, incident reports, and proposals. For example, a problem-solving report might look at why a company lost the market share in the third quarter. The report would then make recommendations on how to increase the market share. A formal proposal is an analytical report that offers to design and/or supply a product or service. It might also be called a feasibility study—a report that analyzes whether a particular course of action is doable and/or desirable. A business proposal, a report that seeks support and funding for a business enterprise, is a type of feasibility study. In a university context, a formal proposal might apply for funding for a certain research project.

Each type of the report has a specific purpose and specific elements to include. A typical type of the informative report and a typical type of the analytical report are elaborated respectively in Table 6.1 and Table 6.2., which illustrates the distinctive differences between the two types of reports.

Table 6.1 An example of informative reports

Report Type or Name	Purpose(s)	Elements to Include
Progress	Explain the status of a project, describing work completed, work in progress, work to do, current or anticipated problems, expected date of completion.	Background, work completed, work in progress, problems, target completion date(s)

Table 6.2 An example of analytical reports

Report Type or Name	Purpose(s)	Elements to Include
Proposal	Persuade the audience to take a course of action.	Letter of transmittal, abstract or executive summary, table of contents, list of illustrations, introduction, background, plan, schedule, personnel, budget

6.2 Report Components

A long report typically includes three sections: front material (the cover page, title page, table of contents, illustrations list, executive summary), text material (the introduction, body, conclusion), and back material (the references, appendices, glossary).

The Transmittal

Whether being distributed digitally or presented in person, reports are always accompanied by an introductory message called a transmittal. The transmittal accompanies the report but is not part of the report itself. Transmittals are written using the direct strategy and discuss what the report is about and why it was written. They may introduce the main points of interest within the report. The message may be in the form of a letter, especially for formal reports going to an outside audience, but it may also be an email or a memo if you are transmitting the report within your organization. The more formal the report, the more formal the transmittal is.

Front Material

Front material consists of pages that come before the report text. Front material may include a cover, an attractively designed front piece for formal reports. The cover page informs the readers what the title of your report is. It provides the name of the organization developing the report, the name of the writer(s), the date, and the persons and/or organization receiving the report.

A title page will contain some or all of the following:

- the report name;

- the person or organization submitting the report;
- the name of the individual and/or organization receiving the report;
- the date when the report is submitted;
- the copyright.

Some reports contain an abstract, a brief distillation of the report's content. Scientific or technical reports often contain abstracts. Descriptive abstracts simply describe the information in the report without offering an interpretation. Informative abstracts summarize key results and offer interpretations.

The table of contents is an outline of the report that provides readers with the location of major categories and subcategories of information. Obviously, a table of contents must contain accurate pagination.

The list of illustrations shows all tables, figures, and maps. It appears on its page and is not part of the table of contents. Tables are generally listed and numbered separately from other figures. All other figures (charts, graphs, maps, photographs) are listed sequentially as they appear in the report.

An executive summary presents the most important elements of a report in a condensed form so a busy manager can glean the report's most critical informative points. As with any summary, an executive summary includes the essential information of the report, is 15% to 20% of the length of the report, and should be able to be read independently from the report. For longer executive summaries, informational headings should be used. Executive summaries are objective and must accurately summarize all essential information, such as the purpose, scope, problems investigated, findings, recommendations, and/or conclusion. A well-constructed executive summary often makes reading the entirety of the report unnecessary.

Text Material

The main text material consists of the major sections of any report you create: the introduction, body, and conclusion. The main text pages are numbered starting with 1 and continuing through the end of the report.

The introduction orients the reader. It includes background information explaining the context of the report and defines the report's limitations. It may provide an overview of the report's organization, sources or methodology used to conduct research, definitions of key terminology, authorization for writing the report, and the report's purpose or significance.

Reports are broken into sections or chapters defined by headings. Headings are organized by hierarchy. First-level headings name major topics. Second-level headings subdivide information under a first-level heading. Third-level headings further subdivide information. Headings may be informative or descriptive. Informative headings can be written as questions or summaries, but they are most effective when they are limited to four to eight words. Descriptive headings name topics. Discussion (or findings) is the longest section of your report. Discuss the data you have collected or compiled. Also provide your analyses, interpretations, and important findings. Discuss advantages and disadvantages of potential solutions to a problem.

In the various sections of a report, information is often cited using a formal citation system. Academic reports use discipline-specific citation systems, such as MLA for the humanities, APA for the social sciences, or CSE for the sciences. Many organizations use the Chicago Manual of Style (CMS) as their guide for citing, which employs footnotes or endnotes accompanied by a list of references in the report's back matter.

All reports must have an ending. A summary is a recap of the report's findings. Conclusions explain how the data in the findings relate to the original problem named in the report's introduction. Conclusions never contain new information because they aim to sum up the report's details. Some reports end with recommendations which provide solutions to the problem the report addresses or suggestions for future actions. Sometimes report conclusions and recommendations appear in the same section. For example:

- More than 80% of pet owners delay prophylactic dental treatment for their pets, citing costs as the deterrent. (Finding)
- Current high costs for prophylactic pet dental treatment are leading to more costly and serious pet health issues and unhappy pet owners. (Conclusion)
- Develop alternate fee structures for prophylactic dental treatment. (Recommendation)

Back Material

The back material is the section of a report that contains details referred to, but not fully included, in the text material. Typical sections are the references and appendices. References contain a list of the sources cited or consulted in the writing of the report, using a formal citation system. Appendices are supplemental to the body of the report and are labeled 1, 2, 3, and so on when more than one appendix is needed. Appendices are reserved for lengthy or highly detailed portions of a report that readers may not want to read in detail. Back material may also include a glossary.

6.3 Procedures of Creating Reports

6.3.1 Planning Your Report

Before starting work on a report you must know why it is needed, and have clear instructions or terms of reference, stating exactly what the report is to be about and setting limits to its scope. Analyzing your audience is important. Identify your readers as clearly as possible so that you can cater to their needs, including a distribution list in your report, and compose a covering letter or memorandum to go with the report. And you must know when the report is required so that you can decide how much time can be devoted to each of the four stages in composition: to thinking, to planning and collecting information, to writing, and to checking and if necessary revising your work. The deadline also helps you to decide on the depth of treatment that should be achievable. Even when working only for yourself, you must consider what you need to do and then allocate your time. Effective time management involves working to a timetable so that you can meet the deadlines imposed by others or by yourself.

Prepare a Topic Outline

Make concise notes as you think of topics that may be included in your report. As an aid to thinking, try to anticipate questions that will be in the minds of your readers. Readers will expect relevant information, well-organized and clearly presented—with enough explanation. For example:

---

1. *Introduction*

What is the problem?

How did you become aware of it?

Why is it of interest to the readers of this report?

2. *Methods*

How did you obtain the information, related to this problem, included in this report?

(Continued)

> 3. *Results*
>
> What did you find?
>
> 4. *Discussions*
>
> What do you make of your findings?
>
> How do they relate to previous work?
>
> 5. *Conclusions*
>
> What do you conclude?
>
> 6. *Summaries*
>
> What does all this mean, in a few short sentences?
>
> 7. *Acknowledgements*
>
> Who financed the work?
>
> Who contributed ideas, information, or illustrations?
>
> 8. *References*
>
> How can I obtain a copy of each of the sources cited in your report?

Number the Sections of Your Report

In technical writing, especially, to facilitate cross-referencing, the parts of a long document can be identified by decimal numbering (point numbering) in both the text and the table of contents. In using this method, no headings are centered. The first section heading is numbered 1. The first subheading in this section is numbered 1.1 and the next 1.2, etc., and minor headings below the first subheading 1.1 are numbered 1.1.1, 1.1.2, etc. If decimal numbering is used, normally it should not go beyond two points. An alternative to numbering paragraphs decimally is to signpost them by letters, (a), (b), etc., but if used with the decimal numbering of section headings, this can be confusing to readers. So it is probably best to keep small letters for successive items in lists, and if it is necessary to number the paragraphs, number them consecutively throughout, and not number the headings.

However, in most business documents, it is not necessary to number either headings or paragraphs. Instead, in a hierarchy of headings, it is necessary. With a word processor, main headings could be in capitals and centered, second-order headings in capitals but not centered, third-order headings in bold, and fourth-order headings in italics. For most purposes, three grades of headings are enough.

6.3.2 Writing Your Report

A formal report has a more formal style of writing and structure than most business and professional writing. For example, a formal report doesn't use contractions. Sentences and paragraphs are shorter than in academic writing but a bit longer and more polished than in most business and professional writing.

Report formats vary somewhat with an organization's style, but a common structure is the following:

1) Front matter or preliminary parts (with pages in Roman numerals).

   a) Cover Page (optional): no page number;

   b) Title Page: Page I, but the page number is not printed;

   c) Letter of Authorization or Memo of Authorization (if the report was commissioned): Page II, with the page number printed;

   d) Letter of Transmittal or Memo of Transmittal (always): usually Page III, with the page number printed;

   e) Table of Contents (you do not need to list the TOC in the table of contents): usually Page IV, with the page number printed;

   f) List of Figures and List of Tables (also called "Table of Figures" and "Table of Tables"): usually Page V, with the page number printed;

   g) Executive Summary: usually Page VI, with the page number printed.

2) Body (with pages in Arabic numerals).

   a) Introduction: Page One, usually with a printed page number ("1") depending on the style;

   b) Background (for a long report): with the page number printed;

   c) Methodology or Mode of Analysis: with the page number printed;

   d) Data and Analysis: with the page number printed;

   e) Conclusions: with the page number printed;

   f) Recommendations: with the page number printed.

3) Back matter (with pages in Arabic or Roman numerals depending on the style).

Note: If Arabic numerals are used, continue the page numbering from the body of the report. If Roman numerals are used, start the numbering from "I".

a) Appendices (labeled, for example "Appendix A"): with the pages numbered;

b) Notes: with the pages numbered;

c) Reference List (with parenthetical citations, use the title "Works Cited" or "References", depending on the documentation style chosen; with footnotes, a section entitled "Bibliography" is optional): with the pages numbered.

In the following, how to write a report will be illustrated part by part according to the natural sequence.

The Front Cover

Include some or all of the following information on the front cover: (a) the name of the organization (and of the division of the organization) responsible for producing the report, and its full postal address; (b) an alphanumeric reference number of less than 33 characters, unique within the organization, which identifies the report and the organization—and should be repeated at the top right-hand corner of every page; (c) the date of issue or the date when completed and ready for reproduction, as appropriate; (d) the title, and if necessary a subtitle; (e) the name(s) of the author(s). If more than one person contributed to the work, their names should be in alphabetical order, or in an order that reflects each person's contribution, or in an order determined by national custom.

Depending upon some rules, the front cover may also include a summary, a distribution list (usually in alphabetical order), the security classification, or a statement relating to confidentiality.

The Title Page

The title comes first, followed immediately by the subtitle and then by the name(s) of the author(s). The abstract or summary may also be included on the title page, or it may be on the next page immediately before the introduction. It is worth giving a lot of thought to the choice of a good title. Its purpose is to inform and to attract the attention of all those who might benefit from reading either the whole report or just the selected parts.

The title should be concise but unambiguous, and it should give a clear indication of the subject and scope of the work. Keywords (words likely to be used in indexes) should be included in your title. Bear in mind its importance and check that it is sufficiently direct and informative. Delete any superfluous words (for example "Aspects of" "A study of" "An inquiry into").

The Abstract or Summary

Although brief, the summary must include your main findings, conclusions, and recommendations, because apart from the title, this is all that some readers will actually read. Ensure that the summary is complete, interesting, and informative without reference to the rest of the report. Write in complete sentences, using words that will be understood by all those for whom your report is intended. In a published report, the summary may be called an abstract. Editors of journals state the maximum number of words to be used in preparing the abstract (usually less than 300).

This section of the report, whether it is called an abstract or a summary, can be written only when the report is otherwise complete. The most effective order will depend on your purpose. If the report is for information only, you may begin by stating a problem and end by saying what has been done about it; if the report is for a committee that is expected to make decisions, you may begin with recommendations.

The Table of Contents

If you think a table of contents would help your readers, list all the main headings, and perhaps also the subheadings, with the same wording and in the same order as in the report, and the page numbers. If you have used decimal numbers for headings, or headings and paragraphs, these should also be included in the table of contents. Alternatively, if all paragraphs are numbered consecutively (not the headings), paragraph numbers should be used on the contents page and in cross-references in the text, instead of page numbers.

The Introduction

The report should begin with a clear statement of the purpose and scope of the work, or the terms of reference, and include a clear statement of the problem (if there is one) and any background information needed to help readers to appreciate why any question you are trying to answer is important. If you have included an abstract or summary before this introduction, do not repeat here things that should properly be in the summary. A clear, concise, and interesting beginning may encourage readers to continue reading. Write in straightforward non-technical language, as in the summary, bearing in mind that some readers will read only the title, summary and introduction, and any conclusions or recommendations. All readers should be able to understand those parts of the report in which they are interested, even if some parts can be understood only by specialists.

The Methods

In a scientific or technical report, enough detail should be included to ensure that if the inquiry or investigation were to be repeated by someone else, with appropriate experience, similar data could be obtained. But for most other reports in business, it is sufficient if readers can understand how the information reported was obtained.

The Results

This section, written in the past tense, should provide a factual statement of your findings, supported by any statistics, tables, or diagrams—but do not present information more than once (for example in a table and a graph). Present the results in an effective order (not usually the order in which the work was done), with enough words to give continuity and to help readers to understand—but otherwise without comment. Take care not to start discussing your results in this section. Note also that any tables in the results section should be summarized. If original data are needed by some readers, they may be included in an appendix or made available in some other way.

The Discussion

An objective consideration of the results presented in the previous section, with appropriate reference to any problem raised in the introduction and to relevant work by others, should lead naturally to your main conclusions. Write in the past tense when commenting on what you did. Otherwise, write in the present tense.

Relevant previous work may be mentioned in the introduction, methods, and discussion sections only, but not in other sections, with complete bibliographical details listed in a bibliography or list of references. However, if you cite someone else's work, always make sure you have read the original publication and know exactly what was done, how and with what result. When summarizing other people's work, try to preserve their meaning. Do not rely on abstracts and reviews, in which the original work of others may not be adequately or correctly represented. If you need to quote someone else's exact words, ensure that all the words and punctuation marks are copied correctly, and make clear that you are quoting verbatim, either by using quotation marks or by indentation and an acknowledgement.

The Conclusions

Your conclusions may be listed at the end of the discussion or after a separate heading. They should follow from arguments and evidence included in your report, and provide an effective ending. They should be numbered, to ensure that they are in order and distinct, and each conclusion should be a precise and concise but clear statement.

The Recommendations

If it is within your terms of reference to make recommendations, they should be practicable and should arise directly from your conclusions. They too should be listed as separate, numbered statements advising, for example precisely what should be done, when it should be done, and by whom.

The Acknowledgements

If anyone helped you, either with the work reported or in preparing the report, this should be acknowledged simply and concisely. It is normally sufficient to write "I thank...for..., and...for...", making clear who contributed and what they did. It is not normally necessary to thank colleagues whose contribution was a routine part of their employment and was insufficient to merit their inclusion as co-authors. You may be required to state the source of finance, for the work and the report; and some organizations may require that a statement be included to the effect that any views expressed are not necessarily officially endorsed.

The Bibliography or List of References

Use the heading "Bibliography" if your list includes bibliographical details of published works that you consulted in preparing your report, or that have influenced your thinking, but are not necessarily cited in your report. Use the heading "References" if your list of sources of information or ideas comprises complete bibliographical details of every publication cited in your report, but no others. Care is needed in checking the accuracy of all references, including the spelling of proper names, because each reference is both an acknowledgement of someone else's work and a source of information for the reader. In general, the heading "References" is used in most scientific and technical reports and the heading "Bibliography" in most other business reports.

References may be listed in alphabetical order or in numerical order, depending on how you have cited sources in the text. Recommendations for bibliographical references are also the subject of British and international standards. How bibliographical details are listed must be consistent with the designated rules. Otherwise, look at a recent internal report to find out what is acceptable to your company or organization, or at a recent issue of the journal in which you hope to publish your work.

The Appendices

Details that would be out of place in the body of a report, but which may be required by some readers (for example tables of original data), may be included in an appendix or made available in some other way.

6.3.3　Improving Your Report

When your report is complete, whether it is handwritten or word-processed, think of it as a first draft.

Check Your Manuscript (First Draft)

When checking the manuscript, please confirm whether there is a satisfactory answer to each of the following questions.

1) Is the title page complete?
2) Does the title provide the best concise description of the contents of your report?
3) Is the use of headings and subheadings consistent throughout the report? Are the headings concise?
4) Are the headings on the "Contents" page identical to those used in the report?
5) Are the purpose and scope of the report stated clearly and concisely in the "Introduction"?
6) Has anything essential been left out? Have you answered all the readers' questions?
7) Are your conclusions clearly expressed?
8) Are the paragraphs in each section in the most effective order? Is the connection between paragraphs clear?
9) Are all arguments forcefully developed and taken directly to their logical conclusion?
10) Is there an important point that could be more clearly expressed, or made more forcefully in an illustration?
11) Is each statement accurate, based on sufficient evidence, free from contradictions?
12) Are there any faults in logic or mistakes in spelling or grammar?

13) Could the meaning of any sentence be better expressed? Is each sentence easy to read?

14) Are any technical terms, symbols, or abbreviations sufficiently explained?

15) Are all the words to be emphasized to be printed in italics or in bold?

16) Are you consistent in spelling, and the use of capitals, hyphens and quotation marks?

17) Are all the references accurate, especially the spelling of proper names?

18) Are each table and each illustration referred to, by its number, in the text?

19) Are the headings in the text identical to those in the list of "Contents"?

20) Does the revised report read well and is it well-balanced?

21) Are those who helped you, either with the work reported or in preparing the report, acknowledged and thanked simply and concisely?

22) Is the source of finance for the work and the report stated clearly?

It is not possible to check your manuscript thoroughly by reading it through once or twice. Instead, check one thing at a time.

Prepare Your Typescript

To ensure the standardization of the typescript, the following are some noteworthy points:

1) Use A4 paper.

2) Use Times New Roman (a serif font): 10-point for single spacing or 12-point for one-and-a-half or double line spacing. A sans serif font (for example Arial) may be preferred for headings.

3) Leave a 40 mm margin on the left; and about 25 mm on the right, top and bottom of the page.

4) Do not justify the right-hand margin.

5) Do not indent the first line of the next paragraph.

6) Number the pages at the bottom center or, for a report that is to be printed, number each page at the top right-hand corner.

7) Use a separate page for each table, with at least 40 mm margins. Type the number of the table and the heading immediately above the table.

8) Center section headings at the top of a new sheet; shoulder subheadings with a line to themselves; and shoulder minor headings and, after a full stop, continue on the same line with the next sentence.

9) Use upper case (capitals) only for the initial letter of each sentence, heading, or proper noun.

10) Underline only those words underlined in the manuscript: the titles of publications, the scientific names of species of organisms, words from a foreign language that are not accepted as English words and abbreviations of such words, and the words "either" and "or" when it is necessary to emphasize an important distinction.

11) Type the contents pages when page or paragraph numbers are known. If the paragraphs are numbered, cross-references in the text can be added in the manuscript—but if, as is more usual, only the pages are to be numbered, both the page numbers and the cross-references must be added either after the typescript has been checked or to the proofs.

12) For a printed report, list the legends to the figures at the end of the typescript, after the tables, below the heading "Legends to Figures".

6.4 Meeting Minutes and Agendas

You may be requested to write meeting minutes, which serve as official reports of what occurred at a meeting. The meeting may be a project meeting, a business meeting, a committee meeting, or any type of meeting for which a record is kept. Many organizations take minutes at meetings. It is because organizations need a record of who was present at the meeting and who was absent, what was discussed, what decisions were made, who was supposed to do what action, when, and so on.

6.4.1 Meeting Minutes

To write effective minutes, you should record identification information, which includes the name of the group holding the meeting. State the type of meeting held, that is, whether it is a regular (e.g. weekly) meeting or a special meeting held to address an immediate issue.

You should also indicate the location, date, and time of the meeting.

Record the names of persons who attended the meeting; it is optional to include the names of persons who were expected to attend but were absent. If minutes of the previous meeting are approved or changed, indicate this in the minutes. Include a list of any reports (e.g. auditors' reports, test reports) that were read and accepted.

Indicate all the main topics that were discussed and describe the main points of the discussion. State any decisions made or any other action items taken or to be done regarding the topic discussed.

If the meeting is conducted using formal motions, record any motion that was made (plus the names of those who made and seconded the motion). Also, record whether the motion was approved, rejected, or tabled. Do not record motions that were withdrawn after discussion. Record any votes that were taken for and against a resolution. Indicate the time the meeting adjourned and the location, date, and time of the next meeting. Finally, sign the meeting minutes, as the recording secretary.

The minutes of a meeting must be prepared soon after the meeting so that they can be sent to some higher committee or a parent body while the points raised in the discussion and the conclusions reached are still fresh in their minds. These minutes provide a concise record of the business conducted, for those present at the meeting and for anyone else who may need to refer to them.

6.4.2 Formats of Minutes

There are many templates online for writing up minutes, but they all follow roughly this format:

- **a letterhead or heading** for the organization the group works for;
- **date and place of the meeting**;
- **time the meeting is to begin**;
- **attendance**;
    - ◇ Members present: If a member is present but arrives late, then record the time that person arrived: "James Turner (6:15)". Similarly, if a person leaves before the meeting is over, mark the time he or she left. Also, indicate who was chairing the meeting: "Sam White (chair)". You could also give the titles of the other chief officers at the meeting: "Jerry Preston (treasurer)".

- ◆ **Absent**: those who didn't make the meeting and didn't let anyone know they were not attending.
- ◆ **Regrets or Excused** (sometimes included in minutes): members who have let the group know in advance they can't make the meeting.

- **recording secretary** (the minute-taker's name);
- **time the meeting began** ("Call to order"): This may not be the same time as was scheduled.
- **approval of the agenda**: At this stage, with the approval of the group, agenda items can be added.
- **approval of the minutes from the previous meeting**: The previous minutes should have been sent to all members several days before the meeting. This is an opportunity to fix possible errors in the previous minutes.
- **reports from group members**, such as the treasurer's or executive director's report;
- **other business**;
- **new business**;
- **adjournment**, including time of adjournment.

Minutes can be in a bulleted or numbered format or paragraphs. Minutes are usually written using full, grammatically correct sentences. They can be in the past tense ("Sam moved that..."), which is the most common, or present tense ("Sam moves that..."). Depending on the formality of the meeting, the minutes will use full names ("Sam Malkin") or first names ("Sam"). Minutes should be as brief as possible while still capturing all the important decisions made at the meeting and the gist of the discussion that led up to these decisions. Most word-processing programs include built-in templates for minutes, and the internet offers a wealth of examples of minutes in many different formats.

Another useful way of structuring the action parts of your minutes is

- topic,
- discussion,
- decision, and
- action (what action, who is to do it, and when it should be complete).

Sometimes, the last item (action) is copied into a separate document called an action list, and this list is distributed to members as a reminder of upcoming responsibilities.

Once the minutes are written and edited, they should be distributed to all members of the group. The following illustrates the layout of the minutes of a committee meeting:

Name of Organization   TC/21/2021

MINUTES
of the meeting of the
TRAINING COMMITTEE

Held at: place, time, day and date of the meeting

PRESENT
Name (Chair), and names of others in alphabetical order

Apologies for absence: names of those who sent apologies

MINUTES
A statement confirming that the Minutes of the meeting held on...(reference No...., circulated on...) were approved as a correct record and signed.

SECRETARY'S REPORT
This may be supported by a concise document with a reference number.

The next minute, starting with a subject heading, is a concise summary of the discussion on this subject and ends with a statement indicating exactly what was decided. This statement begins either with the word:

AGREED...a statement of what was decided, including the terms of reference if a report is required, or before a resolution with the word:

RESOLVED...
Action by: The name of the person who is to take the action required, and the date by which an oral or written report is expected.

DATE OF THE NEXT MEETING
The next meeting will be held at...(place), at...(hour), on...(day and date).

Finally, if your report is being written by a team, you will be taking minutes, so you should know how to do this.

6.4.3 Agendas

A team meeting begins with an agenda, a list of what the members will discuss. So, before a meeting, the secretary and the person who is to chair the meeting agree on the subjects to be discussed, concerning current priorities and the time available, and decide the order in which they are to be discussed. The agenda is sent out to all attendees well before the meeting, so they can suggest changes or additions to what is discussed, and so they can get ready by researching the topics or preparing a presentation. The following is an agenda:

ABC Corp.
FINANCE COMMITTEE MEETING
Lake Room
Monday, September 6, 2021, 9:00 A.M.

AGENDA

Ⅰ. Call to Order
Ⅱ. Approval of the Agenda
Ⅲ. Minutes
      a. Approval of minutes of August 15, 2021
      b. Items arising from minutes (if any)
Ⅳ. Treasurer's Report
Ⅴ. Director's Report
Ⅵ. Other Business
      a. Corporate reorganization for expansion
      b. Date for the annual general meeting
      c. Candidates for the finance committee
      d. Date of the next committee meeting
Ⅶ. New Business
Ⅷ. Adjournment

6.5 Executive Summaries

Academic journal articles can have summaries (often short paragraphs). But in business, an executive summary is usually for a report. The executive summary (sometimes called an abstract) gives the entire body of the report in a nutshell. An executive summary is simply a very brief (usually one-page) summary. It's part of the report itself and comes either right after the title page or after the table of contents. A well-written executive summary is often the key to whether a report communicates effectively or not. Be sure your executive summary can stand alone. For many people, the executive summary is the only part of your report they'll read.

6.5.1 The Purpose of an Executive Summary

You may think that the purpose of an executive summary is to summarize a report for busy executives. That's only partly true. An executive summary is for all people reading the report. Executives and people with peripheral interest will probably read only the executive summary. Other people interested in the detail will certainly begin with the executive summary and then go to the body of the report itself.

As a result, far more people usually read an executive summary than any other part of a report. And that brings us to a crucial point: An executive summary must be able to stand alone. That is:

- An executive summary shouldn't send readers to the body of the report to find all of the important information. Instead, an executive summary must include and summarize the most important information. If people read nothing but the executive summary, they should know, for example whether you recommend building that parking lot, what the cost would be, and what the key issues are.

- An executive summary mustn't assume readers already know the special terminology and concepts that the report itself explains. Instead, an executive summary must assume readers don't know that special terminology and those concepts.

You may wonder if executive summaries must be only a page or less. No. Some excellent ones are a bit longer—but they have a great layout and usually have a key illustration (such as a graph) that causes the executive summary to exceed a page.

You may also wonder if an executive summary must always stand entirely alone.

For the most part, yes. But it can occasionally point to important but space-consuming information in the body of the report, such as a series of key illustrations or detailed recommendations.

6.5.2　The Parts of an Executive Summary

Here are the most common questions that an executive summary answers (in order):

- Who asked for the report? (Don't get tangled up here with a lengthy history of the project. Save that for the body of the report.)

- What does this report look into? (Be brief—say this part in a couple of sentences, if possible, not a few paragraphs.)

- What's the bottom line? (Put the bottom line as close to the beginning of the executive summary as you can.)

- What was your methodology? (In other words, tell how you went about the project—such as preparing a survey to see if employees want a new parking lot, meeting with the zoning board, etc.)

- What are the most important things in the report? (Assume your readers read only the executive summary—what do they absolutely need to know? For example, you may want to list your key recommendations.)

- What's the structure of the report? (Don't go into detail, but do consider listing the main sections of the report, perhaps with a sentence or two of explanation for each item.)

In fact, you don't need to cover all those things in every executive summary. For example, maybe you don't need to explain who asked for the report or what your methodology was. You can save that material for the body of the report itself. The following is a sample executive summary:

what report looks into ── **Executive Summary**　*main point of the report*

We looked at the performance of your middle managers. We found they're not performing nearly as well as they should be.

headings ── **What We Recommend**

example ── • *Allow good middle managers to fail occasionally.* Your middle managers are afraid to innovate because they know there will be a big penalty for

(Continued)

> failure. For example, one said to us, "Why should I try anything when I'll just get my head chopped off if I'm wrong?" That was a common complaint.
>
> - *Clarify the important responsibilities for each middle manager.* We found too many middle managers who thought their most important responsibilities were administrative, such as getting their weekly status reports done and supervising their people. They didn't understand they needed to think strategically, too.
> - *Reward good performers.* You have no incentive system now. We recommend you create such a system and make sure it rewards the most important responsibilities of your middle managers.
>
> **What We Cover**
>
> - Chapter 1, Clarifying the problem. We explain the problem you asked us to solve and explain the reason it exists.
> - Chapter 2, Our approach. This chapter tells you our methodology for looking into the problems and coming up with our recommendations.
> - Chapter 3, Our data gathering. This chapter gives you the detailed results of our surveys and other data we looked at.
> - Chapter 4, Interviews with your staff. In this chapter, we give you the detailed results of our interviews with your vice presidents, middle managers, and other selected staff.
> - Chapter 5, Recommendations. We give you the recommendations for your company as a whole and for each division.

bulleted paragraphs with italicized headings

first person

the structure of the report

6.5.3 The Tips for Preparing an Executive Summary

Keep in mind the following tips when you're preparing your executive summary:

Get to the Point

Readers want to know, right away, the answers to these questions: What did you look into? And what did you find? And they want to know that in the first few sentences. How long does the sample executive summary above take to get to the bottom line? How helpful is that?

Avoid Unnecessary Jargon

What if you explain a lot of special terminology in the body of the report? Can you assume the readers of your executive summary will know those terms? No. You have to write your executive summary as though it's the very first thing your readers look at. It usually is.

Use Plain English

Especially be sure to use the first person (usually *we*).

Use a Good Layout

Some writers want to say so much in an executive summary that they sacrifice the layout—getting rid of white space so they can jam more words onto the page. However, headings are crucial to executive summaries, and bullets are often appropriate. Bulleted paragraphs with italicized headings are especially useful in executive summaries.

Use Examples

Some writers also feel so constrained to keep an executive summary short that they make it entirely abstract. An example or two in your executive summary may be the most memorable part of it.

Consider Using Illustrations

If your report has a key illustration, consider putting it in the executive summary (as well as in the body of the report).

6.6 Proposal Reports

Proposal reports can be informal or formal, depending on the complexity of the proposal. For example, a proposal seeking grant funding may be a page or two or quite long. A business-plan proposal can be dozens or even hundreds of pages long.

Proposals may be solicited (as when a granting agency asks for proposals) or unsolicited (you have generated the proposal yourself, perhaps to seek capital funding). Proposal reports—called briefing notes—are a big part of government decision-making. A feasibility study is also a type of proposal report. The most common proposal report, however, is written in response to a "request for proposal" or RFP. An RFP is a solicitation made by an organization or company interested in purchasing a product, service, or other assets.

In general, a proposal will have most or all of the following elements:

- benefits, results, and feasibility of your proposed project (this section will include enough background to put the proposal in context);
- the report audience—to whom the report is addressed (e.g. a funder, a decision-maker);
- your method and plan;
- a tentative schedule or timeline or a summary of steps;
- your qualifications to do the proposed project;
- what the proposal will cost and resources needed;
- the graphics, pictures, tables, and sources that will be used;
- other supporting information (e.g. the bibliography, list of consultants, or stakeholders).

6.6.1 Briefing Notes

A briefing note provides a government official with very concise background information on a possible policy position and, often, a policy recommendation. Briefing notes follow this general style:

- issue (topic, purpose);
- background;
- current status;
- key considerations;
- options;
- conclusions and recommendations.

An example of a briefing note follows:

File No.: 016789237

Date: February 26, 2018

BRIEFING NOTE FOR THE SUPERINTENDENT OF PUBLIC INSTRUCTION:
AMENDMENTS TO HEALTH EDUCATION IN OHIO SCHOOLS

Summary

From 2009–2017, the Ohio Department of Education has amended Physical Education and Health Sciences in Ohio schools in response to growing rates of obese and overweight children in America.

To reduce the rate of obese and overweight children, the U.S. Department of Health recommends children consume at least five servings of fruits and vegetables per day; however, a study by the Department of Education in 2015 showed none of the Ohio children surveyed consumed five servings of fruits and vegetables per day.

Fewer than 18% of Ohio schools currently offer after-school workshops and brochures to teach both parents and children about eating and cooking more nutritiously.

After-school parent/child workshops and information brochures will cost the Department of Education an extra 3% of its current budget, but this will save the state dollars in the future, as health issues related to obesity cost the state between $730 million and $830 million annually.

Issue

To help prevent obesity in both children and adults, the Ohio Department of Education reformed Health Sciences and Physical Education studies in the state curricula. However, to combat the rise of obesity effectively, schools as well as parents need to participate. Thus, we propose that Ohio schools offer after-school healthy-living workshops to parents and children and distribute brochures to parents to help children make nutritious food choices inside and outside of the home.

Background

Up to 84% of American children do not get enough physical activity to maintain healthy bodies and minds (National Health Interview Survey, 2014/2015).

The Ohio Department of Education recommends 10% of instructional time in

(Continued)

classrooms should be dedicated to physical activity (Ohio Department of Education, 2010).

Over 33% of American children and youth are overweight and approximately 15% are obese (Ohio Department of Health, 2010).

Five or more servings of fruits and vegetables per day substantially decrease the risk of obesity in children and youth (National Health Interview Survey, 2013).

59% of American children and youth consume fewer than five servings of fruits and vegetables per day (NHIS, 2013).

Current Status

The Department of Education now requires students from kindergarten to Grade 9 to participate in 30 minutes of physical activity each day and students from Grade 10 to Grade 12 to complete 150 minutes of physical activity per week.

The Health Education curriculum has also been amended to teach and encourage children to develop better eating habits and make informed, practical food choices. However, Health Education in school is not enough, and parents must encourage good nutrition at home.

Fewer than 18% of schools have a policy or guideline in place, through workshops and brochures, to help parents promote healthy choices. However, the programs do prove to be effective where they are implemented.

Key Considerations

To implement after-school programs and distribute brochures will cost the Department of Education only 3% of its current budget.

Health issues and losses in economic productivity that are related to inactivity cost Ohio approximately between $730 million and $830 million annually (National Institute of Health, 2015).

Economically, Ohio would save $49.4 million if physical activity and healthy eating were increased by only 10% by 2010 (Ohio Department of Health, 2010).

If lifestyle choices can be implemented into children's daily routines while they are still growing, developing, and forming habits, then these same children will grow up to be

(Continued)

> healthier adults who know how to make good choices about food and exercise. Schools and parents must work together to combat this growing problem, so, by offering after-school workshops and brochures, schools can help parents reaffirm healthy living practices that are taught in the classroom.
>
> Originator's name and phone #: Carly Vickers, (555) 555–9898

6.6.2 Formal Proposals

Formal proposals are often the response to an RFP from an organization. The report writers analyze the data, make a proposal, and then explain why their proposal should be accepted or funded.

For example, suppose a university wants to make the campus more environmentally friendly. The university might issue an RFP asking campus members and/or non-members to propose ways to reach the RFP's goal: a more eco-friendly campus. Each submitted proposal would be read and assessed, and successful proposals would be approved and perhaps funded.

When you write your proposal, you will need to keep in mind the following issues:

- Is your proposal feasible with current technology (assuming you are choosing a reality-based topic)? If new technology is needed, can it be invented within a reasonable period?
- Has your proposal been done elsewhere? What were the results (success or failure)?
- What will your proposal cost the client? Can your client afford this? Are there external budget issues that also need to be considered, such as possible government funding restrictions or grants?
- Is your proposal likely to meet with approval by the target readers?
- Are there any legal or regulatory issues to take into account?

In a formal proposal, the division into the front matter, body, and back matter is usually followed.

Chapter 6 Reports

Front Matter

- **Title Page**: Page 1 (actually, the Roman numeral "I") but the number is not printed.

- **Letter** or **Memo of Authorization** (the RFP itself): This section may or may not appear in the proposal report depending on an organization's style. If it is included, as front matter it would be numbered II, in Roman numerals, with the page number printed. From here on, all page numbers are printed.

- **Letter** or **Memo of Transmittal**: This introduces your submission of the proposal. Use a memo if the issuers of the RFP are within your organization (e.g. a university grants committee). If there is a letter or memo of authorization, this would be Page III. If there is no authorization document, then it would be Page II.

- **Table of Contents**: Page III or IV, depending on whether there is an authorization document.

- **List of Figures**: Page IV or V.

- **List of Tables**: This section could be on the same page as figures or a separate page if there are many tables.

- **Executive Summary** or **Summary** or **Abstract**: This section summarizes the entire report, Page VI or VII. In some proposal report formats, the summary goes after the letter or memo of transmittal.

- **Glossary**: A glossary of technical terms is optional and most often found in engineering and scientific proposals; it would be Page VII or VIII. The glossary may also go ahead of the executive summary, or even in the back matter section, depending on your organization's report style.

Body

- **Introduction**: As this is the beginning of the text of a report, the page number is "1", in Arabic numerals, printed. As part of the introduction, you may include the following:

    ◆ Purpose: why the report is being written (for example in response to an RFP) and why this proposal will solve the problem.

    ◆ Background: enough detail to put the report's proposal in context.

    ◆ Scope: what the report will cover—the boundaries.

- **Project description**: how you propose to address the topic, including
    - how you will show that your project is feasible;
    - the specific expected benefits;
    - negative consequences of not doing as you propose;
    - obstacles to your proposal, recognition of problems in achieving your goal.
- **Methodology**: how you did your investigation; how you conducted your survey if you have one.
- **Qualifications**: you and/or your team's qualifications/expertise to investigate this topic.
- **Resources**: what is needed to make the proposal feasible, e.g. institutional funding, access to organizational resources, a source of raw materials, and so on.
- **Projected timeline**: a detailed timeline, probably using a Gantt chart, on how long you will need to finish the project, with timelines for each stage of the project.
- **Budget**: an itemized, detailed estimate of costs to finish the proposed project, in a table format.
- **Conclusions**: what you are proposing and why it is both feasible and desirable.
- **Recommendations**: the summary of what you are proposing in the bullet list format; each list item begins with an action verb ("improve" "allow" "incorporate"). This may be included in conclusions and therefore not as a separate section. If there is only one recommendation, then don't use the bullet list format.

Back Matter

- **Appendices**: additional material, such as the questions for a survey. Appendix A would be the survey itself; Appendix B would be the data from the survey, in the table format. Since this is a back matter, you could switch to Roman numerals, starting with "I". However, as with the analytical report, this change of number style is optional.
- **Notes**: If the report's notes are within the body of the report, at the bottom of pages, this section is not necessary.
- **References**: works cited in one of the accepted reference formats (MLA, APA, CSE), if you have cited resources.

6.7 Surveys

Not all reports have surveys, but a basic knowledge of how to create a survey can still be useful in report writing. Part of a report, either informal or formal, might be a market survey or questionnaire to add empirical support to the report writers' conclusions. To elicit useful information, the questions on these surveys must be as meaningful and objective as possible.

Meaningful questions are concrete and specific and elicit concrete and specific answers. For example:

> —Did you find the website reader-friendly?
>
> —Yes. / No. / Don't know. / No opinion.

This question will not make sense to someone not familiar with the idea of reader-friendliness. Better questions would be the following:

> Did you find the website's font large enough to read easily?
>
> Did you find the website's layout attractive?
>
> Did you find the website easy to navigate?
>
> Did you find the information easy to find on this website?

These questions will elicit more concrete and specific answers and are more meaningful and therefore more useful.

The other problem is bias in survey questions—questions that aim to elicit a specific answer. For example:

> We are calling to ask you two quick questions because we are concerned that the Regional District sewage project will continue to flush toxic chemicals and pharmaceuticals into the ocean even after treatment.

Who would want to flush toxic chemicals into the ocean? So a question like that is aiming for the answer the surveyors want. It is a leading, biased approach. A more objective statement might be this:

> Are you concerned that, although the Regional District eliminates 99% of toxic chemicals and pharmaceuticals before sewage is sent into the ocean, treatment does not eliminate 100% of these pollutants?

Another example of a leading question might be this:

> Do you support wasteful spending by the government on welfare?

Who would support wasteful spending on anything? Remove "wasteful" and the question becomes more objective and the responses more meaningful.

Survey questions can take many forms. They can be "yes/no" responses for relatively black and white questions. These are known as "closed-ended" questions because they aim to elicit a specific answer. An "open-ended" question aims for a more detailed and nuanced response, such as "How did you feel after your accident?" "What do you think caused the accident?" Survey questions are often asked using the Likert scale, which runs from "strongly disagree" to "strongly agree", with several gradations in between. Likert-scale surveys are often presented as statements rather than questions. Likert-scale questions are "closed-ended" because they limit the response.

For example, let's say you were reporting on the desirability of a new bus route in your city, and you asked 1,000 randomly selected adults for their opinions on this topic. The result for a five-part Likert-scale survey might look like this:

Issue: Should our city approve a new bus route from downtown to Orange Island?

Table 6.3 New bus route survey results

Strongly Disagree	Disagree	Neutral	Agree	Strongly Agree
57	169	103	563	108

What you've created is a table, and you could put it in your report. But tables are not as easy to interpret as graphs.

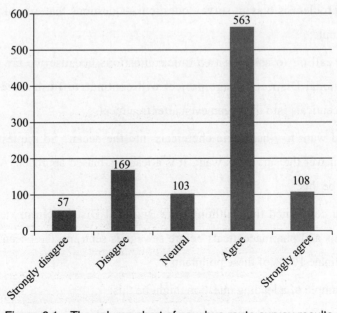

Figure 6.1 The column chart of new bus route survey results

From the graph, it's clear at a glance that more city people favor allowing the new bus route than are opposed.

Another possibility is a pie chart, as in Figure 6.2. Once again, at a glance, it's clear that, in this imaginary survey, a majority of city people favor the new bus route from downtown to Orange Island.

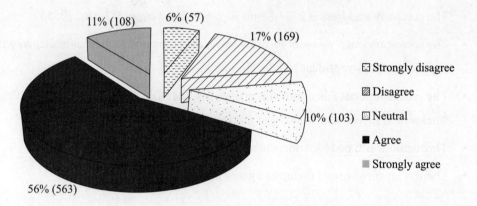

Figure 6.2   The pie chart of new bus route survey results

One final point: Surveys aren't perfect reflections of reality. Even though our New Bus Route Survey showed that a majority of city people favor the new bus route from downtown to Orange Island, another survey with a different sample population might get a different result.

The best surveys are those that include a very large population: the larger the sample, the more likely the survey results will be accurate, or close to accurate.

In general, as we discussed in Chapter 3, when the actual numbers are important, you should use a table format. When the comparison of the numbers is important, use a graph. Once the graphs are ready, you can use them in the body of your report, both to offer data that is easy to interpret and to add color to a page. The table on which the graph is based can go into the report as an appendix.

> **Exercises**

1. *According to the following information, create the first and closing parts of a formal memo on letterhead, using proper formatting and spacing.*
   - The correspondence was sent by Penelope Anderson, the general manager of Terrapin Marmot Figurines, Ltd., on January 24, 2019.
   - The company's address is 2334 South Ripley Road, Terrapin, Texas, 79555.
   - The correspondence was sent to Bill Cleary, the company's financial manager, with a copy to company president Natalie Henstrick.
   - The correspondence is about the possibility that Terrapin Marmot may invest in Rockwallen Investment's family of mutual funds.
   - The memo was typed by Anderson's secretary, Leslie King.
   - There is an enclosure of financial figures for the fall quarter.

2. *You have been asked to do a survey on people's attitudes towards an issue of importance in your city (you choose the issue; it could be anything from parking to overcrowdedness on a certain bus). Think of 10 specific questions, using whatever type of question you prefer (open- or closed-ended questions). Design questions to draw out the views of a sample of 100 citizens on whatever issue you select. Conduct the survey and make a brief report.*

3. *The Campus Committee on Sustainability (CCS) of your university has sent out an RFP for a report to improve the university's eco-friendliness by reducing energy use, curbing carbon emissions, or just generally any project that would make the campus more eco-friendly.*

   Your mission is to come up with a proposal idea, research the topic to determine if it is feasible or not, and then write the proposal. If further research is required to ensure feasibility, then you should include that information as well. Note that, for this assignment, you should write the report as if the proposal is feasible.

   As part of the formal proposal, please create a survey of students. You should use charts from this survey in the body of your report. The survey questions should be in Appendix A, and the data (in the table format) in Appendix B.

Chapter 7
Writing for the Oral Presentation

Never underestimate the power of the oral presentation which plays an important role in your career growth. In a competitive world where professionals are expected to give oral presentations as part of the job, delivering presentations is no longer reserved for high-level CEOs and managers; both employers and employees are required and expected to develop good oral presentation skills to communicate effectively with internal and external audiences. Impressive oral presentations help you to land the job of your dreams, increase your visibility in the workplace, and make you stand out among colleagues.

Communication is the essence of all business transactions and a successful oral presentation leads to effective communication. Oral presentation skills will help you at face-to-face meetings, at network conferences with colleagues, at circumstances where you need to speak with clients and detail a technical topic. Solid presentations motivate and inspire your audience and move your audience to action, helping you to sell your product or service, and attract investors to back your ideas.

In this chapter, you will learn about:

- understanding the oral presentation as a way of communication;
- preparing an audience-targeted oral presentation;
- making an audience-targeted oral presentation.

7.1 Understanding the Oral Presentation as a Way of Communication

Communication is a process by which information, ideas, or feelings are exchanged, transmitted, or conveyed through a common system of symbols, signs, or behavior. Messages will be received successfully through effective communication. In the workplace, effective oral presentations can encourage a healthy working environment and enhance working efficiency by improving internal and external communication.

7.1.1 Making Successful Oral Presentations

To make successful oral presentations, you will need to keep in mind the following issues:

Chapter 7 Writing for the Oral Presentation

- What is a presentation?
- What is the essence of a presentation?
- Does your presentation achieve the communication purpose that you're expecting?

The Definition of Presentation

Presentation is a structured communication based on the actual audience's needs to achieve a certain purpose within a given timeframe, where the overall goals are providing information and promoting ideas.

In the workplace, written and oral presentations are two presentation channels for internal and external communication. Written presentations are good choices to present complicated facts like regulations, reports, proposals, agreements, contracts, etc., while oral presentations are good choices to build agreement, solve conflicts, and establish harmonious relationships between the speaker and the audience. With appropriate support of a written presentation, an oral presentation will allow the speaker to take advantage of both forms.

An oral presentation is much more than just presenting your ideas or delivering a speech. It is about skillful communication relating to the audience—whether the audience is a few people or a large gathering. It is an effective way to direct the audience's attention, receive instant feedback from the audience, answer questions face to face, and adjust ideas according to the audience's reactions.

The Goal of the Oral Presentation

An oral presentation in the workplace is usually a formal, research-based presentation of your work. If you are a sales manager and are responsible to sell products produced by your company, then you may organize your team to give an oral presentation on the progress of your promotion project. If you work with a charity organization, you may give an oral presentation at an annual meeting to share information on its activities, budget, and goals with funders and community members.

Learning how to construct and deliver an effective oral presentation is a useful skill and understanding the goals of the presentation will cultivate your consciousness of your audience. The secret to a successful presentation is to understand that you are communicating with your audience on different occasions for different purposes. If you are a scholar presenting your research findings, if you are a teacher presenting kids' behavior at school, or if you are a manager presenting the progress of a certain project, you are informing. If you are presenting at a workshop or training session, you are teaching or instructing. If you are persuading the potential client to choose your product or service at sales presentations, the goal of your presentation is to persuade or convince. If you are analyzing the problem and working towards a solution with your views and methods, your presentation is trying to make your audience take action.

7.1.2 Avoiding Inappropriate Use of PowerPoint Slides

PowerPoint is the slideshow software created by Microsoft and is widely used for oral presentations. Millions of people use this powerful software for oral presentations every day and it is probably the first presentation software that comes to mind when people are asked to present something. The application of PowerPoint in the workplace has proved to be beneficial, yet inappropriate use of the software will lead to ineffective communication and even become a barrier to successful communication between the presenter and the audience.

Avoid Confusing Oral Presentations with PowerPoint Slides

To make successful oral presentations with the right choice of software, you will need to keep in mind the following issues:

- What visual medium should be chosen to support your oral presentation?
- Is PowerPoint the best choice to support your oral presentation?
- Are there any software that will help you to achieve a better communication effect?

Nowadays, the oral presentation has been at the heart of every business, work, and educational process. You will make many oral presentations in the workplace and learning oral presentation skills is as important as learning written presentation skills. Making an oral presentation means to express ideas or stimulate a brief discussion on a defined topic. Researching, planning, and structuring an oral presentation are similar to the process of writing to present your ideas.

Learning to use visual aids helps you to make a successful oral presentation. Microsoft PowerPoint is getting so popular that many users confuse oral presentations with PowerPoint presentations. In fact, you can choose a variety of presentation software to support your oral presentations and you should avoid confusing an oral presentation with a PowerPoint presentation. For example, Keynote is interactive presentation software designed by Apple

Inc. It is a successful competitor of PowerPoint among Mac OS users, helping presenters to outline presentations, creating engaging and dynamic slides, adding charts and graphs to slides, editing photos, and adding effects to sharpen the presentation, playing videos and movies continuously across slides. Prezi is the software designed to help you to make presentations over the video, and it is an engaging way to keep the personal connection in remote meetings or classrooms, and the video appears right alongside your content. Mind maps, unlimited zooms, interactive and dynamic features, simplicity, and convenience make Prezi a popular online presentation tool.

An oral presentation cannot simply be equated with a PowerPoint presentation. Different pieces of software have different strengths and weaknesses and can serve as a great PowerPoint alternative to help you to make creative and captivating presentations if chosen appropriately.

Avoid Neglecting Communication with the Audience

Heavy workloads, combined with human factors like laziness and procrastination make us anxious to finish coming presentations. Today, the built-in editing tools, embedded add-ins, templates, transitions and animations, text highlighters, and drawing tools offered by software like PowerPoint help presenters to prepare and make presentations quickly. PowerPoint seems to be able to handle whatever you throw at it, like texts, photos, tables, charts, links, videos, etc., and make your slides look professional in appearance. However, the oral presentation should focus on the audience instead of the software.

A smart presenter should guide the audience to identify the core concept of the presentation. The basic purpose of a PowerPoint presentation is to offer visual aids to help presenters to enhance communication effect. Poor application of PowerPoint not only distracts the attention of the audience but also lowers the effect of communication. Furthermore, Microsoft PowerPoint is a powerful and convenient computer tool for making on-screen multimedia presentations, but relying too much on PowerPoint makes you neglect your communication with your audience.

In the workplace, an oral presentation is a kind of communication skill that requires learning and training.

7.2 Preparing an Audience-targeted Oral Presentation

The power of a well-prepared oral presentation can't be ignored. In the workplace, an oral presentation is a form of communication in which ideas and plans are offered, shown, and explained to your audience. On some occasions, you may make oral presentations briefly and informally to whom you work closely with every day. On other occasions, you may make oral presentations formally to upper-level managers. You may also make oral presentations on a new product or service, or a piece of work to your clients or a group of people at a meeting, to your business partners, to professional organizations, or to the general public.

A successful oral presentation is interactive and requires skills of persuasion and influence. To make an oral presentation tailored to the needs of your audience, you will need to keep in mind the following issues:

- What are the basic types of oral presentations?
- How important is your topic to your audience?
- What is the purpose of speaking with your audience?
- What software or other visual media should be chosen to support your presentation?
- How should you organize the information selected for the oral presentation?

7.2.1 Types of Presentations

There are two basic types of oral presentations in the workplace: the informative presentations and the persuasive presentations. Different types of presentations have different purposes. However, most presentations will have elements of both types but primarily aim at one purpose or the other.

Informative Presentations

The purpose of the informative presentation is to transmit specific knowledge, convey certain information, or promote understanding of an idea. Informative presentations are often used to provide people with information about a concept or idea that is new and usually in a logical sequence. The presenters introduce the topic at the beginning, and then provide explanations, directions, or descriptions for the discussion part, and finally restate or conclude the topic. For example, if you are working for the Xiamen Municipal Government and you are asked to make an oral presentation to athletes who will attend the 2022 Xiamen International

Chapter 7 Writing for the Oral Presentation

Marathon before the opening ceremony, you would make an informative presentation. You can introduce the amazing game to the athletes and emphasize the importance of the game to the city; then explain the locations where the game is to be held and detail the specific information about the route, also notify the athletes of the rules and regulations of the game, and offer information about services and medical support along the route. Finally, restate the importance of the game.

Persuasive Presentations

The goal of a persuasive presentation is to convince the audience to believe or do something. For example, you may try to convince your company to fund your project, or you may want your company to approve an expansion overseas. Since the purpose is to persuade the audience to believe something and motivate the audience to take action, the topic is usually introduced with an attention-getting introduction to capture the attention of the audience at the very beginning. A concrete example, an opening story, a surprising fact, a joke, or an anecdote can be used to attract the interest of the audience. Presenters also use visualization to communicate abstract points, to highlight benefits satisfying the need of the audience, to show how ideas, proposals, products, or services will help to resolve the problem. At the end of the presentation, presenters usually repeat major ideas, provide the action steps for the audience to take, and finish the presentation with strong and impactful language.

7.2.2 Strategies for Oral Presentation Preparation

To make a successful oral presentation, you should prepare an audience-targeted presentation based on the following guidelines.

Analyze the Audience

The audience is the key element of a successful presentation and getting to know the audience is fundamental to maximizing the success of any communication. Different audiences have different information needs and different expectations. To make an effective oral presentation, you need to understand what your audience knows and cares about, and then tailor your oral presentation to the needs of your audience appropriately.

Every presentation has its specific audience and every audience is unique. For example, your audience will have different expectations when you make a presentation on the annual budget of a project to your team members, or the CEO of your company because there is some sort of hierarchy that needs to be addressed. The requirements for introducing a new tourism project to the native speaker travelers should be different from the requirements for introducing it to a group of foreigners. And factors related to cultural differences should be taken into account when you talk to foreigners.

An oral presentation without understanding the expectation of your audience will not be powerful. The position in the organization, educational background, cultural background, personal expectation, the level of knowledge about the topic you will deliver, and a lot of other factors are to be considered before structuring the presentation message. Failure to understand your audience and address their needs and interests will hinder your presentation.

Clarify Your Purpose

Besides understanding your audience, you should also figure out the exact purpose of your oral presentation and think about how you want to affect or influence your audience. Without clarifying the purpose of the presentation, you cannot give proper information to your audience.

There are many reasons for giving a presentation. Different reasons lead to different purposes. For example, TED is a non-profit foundation devoted to spreading ideas, and many famous presentations are delivered during TED Talks. TED presenters come from all walks of life, developing and delivering engaging presentations to a good-sized audience to change the attitudes, and even lives of the audience with the power of ideas. When Huawei announced the new HUAWEI P50 Series, Huawei Consumer Business Group made presentations to the public to inform the public that the latest addition to its iconic product is available. The presentation had manifested and hidden purposes. The manifested purpose is to announce a new product while the hidden purpose is to persuade customers into buying the product. Similarly, many presentations have manifested and hidden purposes.

Select an Appropriate Topic

You need to put a lot of thought into selecting the best topic for your oral presentation because a well-chosen topic guides the direction of the discussion. Once you are acquainted with the nature of your audience, narrow down your options and select a topic that your audience will be able to relate to. For example, if your audience consists mainly of first-year

Chapter 7 Writing for the Oral Presentation

students, and you want to make a promotion on an E-learning App, then you need to choose a topic relating to the interest of the kids. However, if your audience consists mainly of parents, a topic relating to the safe and unique online self-study will be more effective. Furthermore, by delving deeper into the circumstances of your audience, you'll be able to modify your topic further for maximum effect. For example, your research helps you to find that a group of your audience consists mainly of parents who are well-educated and have high expectations of their children while another group consists mainly of parents who are not so well-educated and have low expectations of their children. Then you can select different presentation topics tailored to the needs of different audiences.

Choosing the correct topic is the most difficult task for making a presentation. Besides the needs of the audience, the audience's knowledge of the topic and learning potential should be anticipated. Furthermore, the presenter and the audience may have different relationships with the subject. For example, the presenter is familiar with the subject, but the audience is not well-informed or the audience and the presenter are equally informed. And occasionally, when you structure your message, you may find that the topic you have chosen is too large or complex for the time available, and then you will have to go back and review the specific topic you wish to address.

7.2.3 Strategies for Developing an Effective Presentation

Choose Appropriate Software or Other Visual Media

Oral presentations will be creative or interesting if you can choose the right visual medium. Understanding the varieties of oral presentation software and other visual media helps you to choose the right visual medium to support your oral presentation. PowerPoint is very popular in the workplace; it offers creative presentation tools with built-in templates to create oral presentations with images, videos, transitions, and animations. However, sometimes, a combination of visual media is also a good choice. For example, a sales manager of a biopharmaceutical company needs to make an oral presentation on the latest vaccine developed by the company to a group of important clients, then he can use PowerPoint slides to show photographs of experiments made by the vaccine development team, use chalkboards to explain the production line of the vaccine, and use handouts to explain detailed statistics for further understanding.

Undoubtedly, Microsoft PowerPoint has been essential in office jobs nowadays and you will sit through hundreds of presentations in the PowerPoint format in the workplace in your career development. The following discussion will focus mostly on oral presentations prepared with the support of Microsoft PowerPoint.

Structure a Clear, Concise, and Consistent Presentation

An effective structure guides the audience to keep up with you and makes you feel more confident and relaxed when you deliver a presentation. A widely used structure usually consists of three parts: the introduction, body, and conclusion. However, each part of the basic structure can be designed in various ways depending on the context. For example, for the conclusion part, depending on the different actions you want your audience to make after listening to your presentation, you may end your oral presentation with a summary, a review, a solution, or relevant information and resources. The following is a basic structure for you to learn:

Table 7.1 A basic oral presentation structure

Introduction		Introduce the topic.
		Forecast the organization with main points.
		Provide background information if necessary.
Body	First point	State the point.
		Support with explanation and elaboration.
	Second point	State the point.
		Support with explanation and elaboration.
	Third point	State the point.
		Support with explanation and elaboration.
Conclusion		Review or summarize main points.
		Provide possible solutions.
		Provide relevant information or resources.

The following is a presentation example using the basic structure. The presentation is made by the Centers for Disease Control and Prevention. The first slide introduces the topic "Building Confidence in COVID-19 Vaccines Among Your Patients: Tips for the Healthcare Team".

Chapter 7 Writing for the Oral Presentation

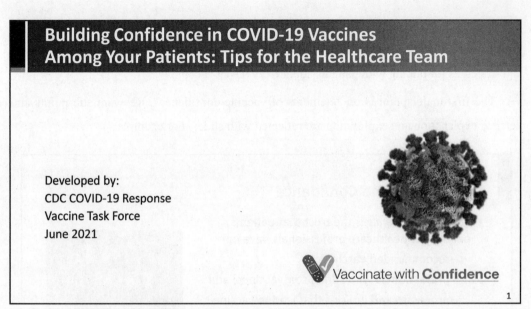

Figure 7.1 Presentation slide 1—Building Confidence in COVID-19 Vaccines Among Your Patients: Tips for the Healthcare Team

The second slide is an overview of the presentation, forecasting the structure of the presentation.

Figure 7.2 Presentation slide 2—Building Confidence in COVID-19 Vaccines Among Your Patients: Tips for the Healthcare Team

After introducing the topic and forecasting the structure of the presentation, the presentation guides the audience, that is, the healthcare team, to understand the topic with concrete information, explaining how to build vaccine confidence among patients. There are three major points: elements of vaccine confidence, strategies for building vaccine confidence, and strategies for talking with patients about COVID-19 vaccine.

The first major point is on "elements of vaccine confidence". Relevant sub-points and detailed explanation and exploration are reflected with slides. For example:

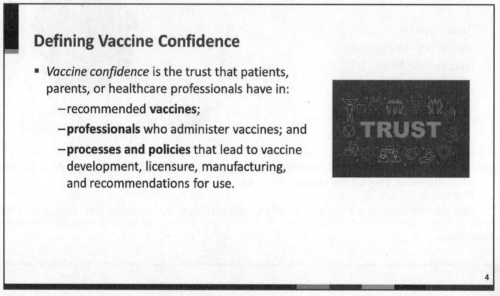

Figure 7.3　Presentation slide 4—Building Confidence in COVID-19 Vaccines Among Your Patients: Tips for the Healthcare Team

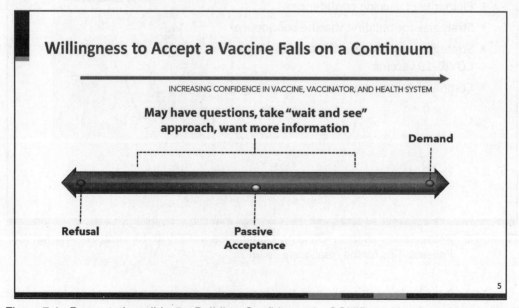

Figure 7.4　Presentation slide 5—Building Confidence in COVID-19 Vaccines Among Your Patients: Tips for the Healthcare Team

The second major point "strategies for building vaccine confidence" is illustrated in detail with slides as follows:

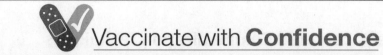

Figure 7.5 Presentation slide 8—Building Confidence in COVID-19 Vaccines Among Your Patients: Tips for the Healthcare Team

Figure 7.6 Presentation slide 9—Building Confidence in COVID-19 Vaccines Among Your Patients: Tips for the Healthcare Team

The third major point talks about "strategies for talking with patients about COVID-19 vaccine". Detailed strategies are explained and elaborated with slides. For example:

Use Patient-centered Communication Techniques

- **Use open-ended questions** to promote dialogue. Ask about readiness to vaccinate and what questions or concerns they may have.
- **Paraphrase** any information shared to show that you have heard and understood it.
- **Praise measures already taken** to protect themselves or their children from COVID-19, like mask wearing and physical distancing. Then **frame** vaccination as a safe and effective way to help protect them and their loved ones from getting COVID-19.
- **Ask for permission** to share more information on COVID-19 vaccines. This will foster openness and connection.

14

Figure 7.7   Presentation slide 14—Building Confidence in COVID-19 Vaccines Among Your Patients: Tips for the Healthcare Team

Help Individuals Find Their Motivation for Getting Vaccinated

- Steer the conversation away from "why not?" and toward the important reasons that matter to them—**their "why"**.
- The reasons that someone may choose to get vaccinated will always be those that are **most compelling to them personally**.
- You may choose to share your reasons for getting vaccinated or discuss common goals you may have, like visiting with family safely.

21

Figure 7.8   Presentation slide 21—Building Confidence in COVID-19 Vaccines Among Your Patients: Tips for the Healthcare Team

Finally, the presentation concludes with slides offering relevant information and resources for further support.

Different topics involve different messages and relevant points. Since different audiences have different needs and expectations for the same topic, the focus of the presentation should be different. For example, as an engineer, when you present to a group of your colleagues on the water-leaking problem of a tunnel under construction, you are presenting to a very narrow audience whose understanding of the problem is similar to you; however, if you present the same topic at a big conference, you may present to a more general audience.

Coordinate Verbal and Visual Parts

The power of your presentation will be greatly enhanced if verbal and visual elements are used appropriately. Software like Microsoft PowerPoint, Prezi, Google Slides, Keynote, PDF helps you to change an average presentation into an attention-grabbing, memorable, effective means of communication. Vivid pictures and photos, dynamic diagrams and graphics, tables organizing and displaying information in rows and columns, charts displaying numerical data, videos, media clips or any other media files can be embedded into a presentation to support or reinforce messages being delivered. Besides software, diversified visual aids like flip charts, overhead projectors, handouts can also be used. The flip chart is an alternative to the pervasive PowerPoint presentation, it is a large board with pieces of paper attached at the top, and it offers a simple tool for presenting information to an audience by turning over one piece of paper at a time. The paper-version visual materials can be prepared before the presentation or supplemented during the presentation. It is also convenient to write and draw on flip charts spontaneously during the presentation. For example, you can write down ideas of the audience, make sketches, draw charts or schemes, write tasks for discussion, and so on when interacting with the audience during the presentation. An overhead projector is an electronic version of a flip chart. Handouts play different roles during the presentation and can be used as a reminder of the content and learning points.

Appropriate integration of verbal and visual dimensions enhances the combined communicative power of words and images, thus greatly improving the effectiveness of a presentation. The following is an example. It is a presentation delivered in June 2020 by Healthcare-Associated Infections Clinical Excellence Commission and the topic is "Coronavirus: COVID-19". A series of pictures is used to emphasize the importance of P2/

N95 respirator fit checks when people are wearing masks. Slides with simple words and vivid pictures help to achieve longer message retention, stronger influence, and better results.

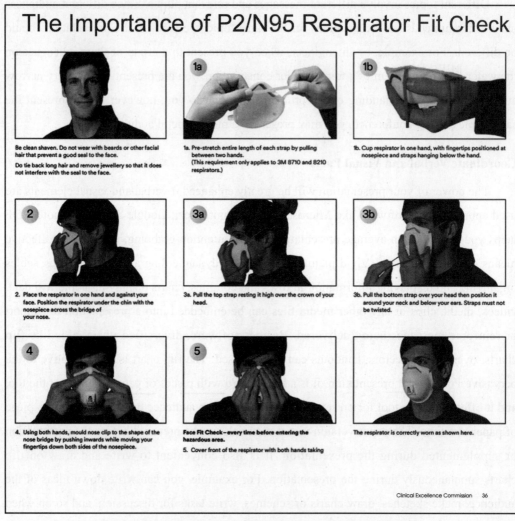

Figure 7.9　Presentation slide 36—Coronavirus: COVID-19

　　Screen after screen of text will make your audience feel bored because text-heavy slides create monotony and redundancy. When Victor C. Uremia who works for Johns Hopkins University School of Medicine, Gregory W. Albers who works for Stanford Stroke Center of Stanford University, and Peter D. Panagos who works for Stroke Network of Washington University School of Medicine are presenting their research findings with the topic "As Time Is of the Essence: Incorporating Recent Guideline Updates to Support Early Recognition and Management of Acute Ischemic Stroke", they use various visual aids like pictures, graphics,

Chapter 7 Writing for the Oral Presentation

tables, and so on to make their abstract explanation of their research findings concrete. The following are some slides taken out of the presentation:

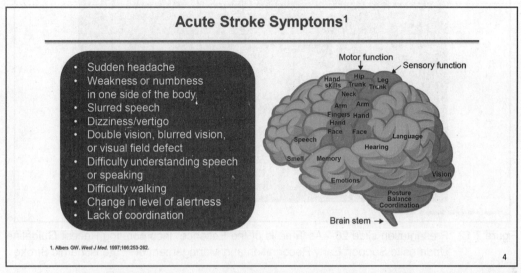

Figure 7.10 Presentation slide 4—As Time Is of the Essence: Incorporating Recent Guideline Updates to Support Early Recognition and Management of Acute Ischemic Stroke

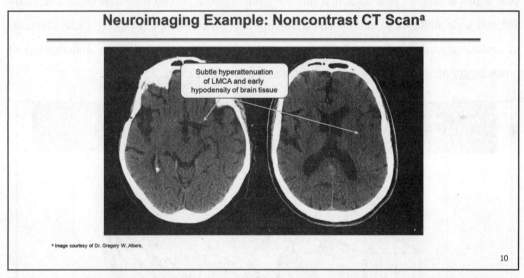

Figure 7.11 Presentation slide 10—As Time Is of the Essence: Incorporating Recent Guideline Updates to Support Early Recognition and Management of Acute Ischemic Stroke

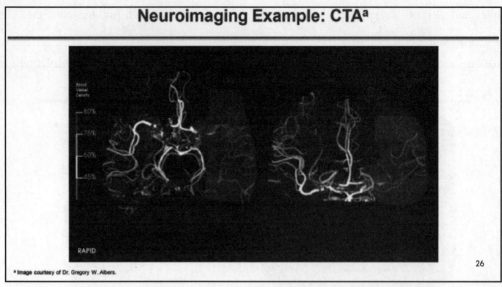

Figure 7.12　Presentation slide 26—As Time Is of the Essence: Incorporating Recent Guideline Updates to Support Early Recognition and Management of Acute Ischemic Stroke

It is important to learn to incorporate relevant and appropriate visual elements into your slides to engage your audience and use your valuable presentation time most efficiently and call your audience to action. The following is another example of using visual elements to replace abstract and complicated messages. The slide illustrates the distribution of groundwater beneath Los Alamos with a clear and concise picture.

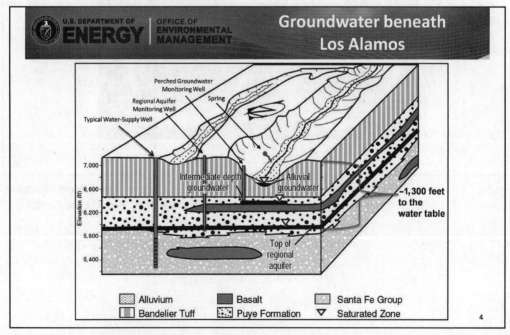

Figure 7.13　Presentation slide 4—Los Alamos National Laboratory's RDX Groundwater Project

7.2.4 Revising Presentation Slides Before Delivery

Revising presentation slides is a necessary step before delivery. A well-prepared presentation with appropriate revision is essential to the successful presentation delivery. Even an excellent presenter who is an expert on the topic should avoid coming to a presentation unprepared. If even one of these rules is broken, the delivery process can be severely hindered. An effective presentation is much more than just presenting ideas, but communicating with the audience.

Successful presenters are successful writers and successful editors. To make an audience-targeted presentation, you need to clarify your key messages and check whether a logical sequence has been established. You also need to check whether the message matches the needs of the audience, and check whether the language and visualization are effectively used. Furthermore, you should check if you have used simple language and a friendly tone to express your ideas. No unfamiliar terms or unexplained acronyms that will hinder the communication between you and the audience should be used.

7.3 Making an Audience-targeted Oral Presentation

Content preparation and delivery of the content form the indivisible whole of a presentation process. No matter how perfectly the structure, content, and design of the presentation are prepared, the delivery of a presentation can make all the difference between a great presentation and a poor one. Good delivery skills are necessary for anyone who wants to communicate successfully to get career or business opportunities.

7.3.1 Preparing Before Presentation Delivery

Access the Presentation Scene

Before structuring the presentation message, you need to understand the scene in which you will communicate. As a general rule, matching slide backgrounds with the room in which you're presenting can be very effective, allowing eyes to be drawn to the content of the presentation, not on the slides themselves. The size of the audience, the relationship between the presenter and the audience, the location of your presentation and the available equipment should all be considered. The following are some images of presentation rooms, designed to serve different scales of the audience:

Figure 7.14　Some presentation rooms

Presenters also need to arrange or request technology in advance of the conference. You can ask the conference organizers what technology will be available.

Control Your Presentation Time

　　Good timing helps you to keep your audience engaged. Before making a presentation, it is helpful to figure out how much time you will have for your presentation. At the beginning of the delivery, professional presenters often make the rules clear to the audience and emphasize how much time there is for the presentation. Talking too long may ruin an otherwise successful presentation, since your audience may lose patience if you don't limit your time. Usually, it is up to the presenter to decide the time frame of the presentation; however, on some occasions, the time frame is determined by the audience or the organizer; then the structure of the presentation will have to be developed in a way that key messages of the presentation can be delivered within the time limit.

　　After designing and developing a presentation, it is necessary to rehearse before delivering it. Rehearsing is essential to help you to make sure that enough time will be spent on the presentation, and avoid spending too much time at the beginning and rushing at the end. Rehearsing also helps you to decide how much time to be spent on each major point or each slide based on the time allotted to the presentation. You can also rehearse a presentation by actually delivering it in an empty room or with a few friends or colleagues who can monitor the pace of your presentation and the time you take, and give you constructive feedback.

7.3.2 Delivering Presentations with Skills

Learning some oral presentation skills helps you to involve your audience in your presentation and increase the possibility of effective communication; also increase the likelihood of driving your audience to take action and realize your purpose, whether the purpose is to persuade your audience to accept ideas and concepts, make changes, take action, buy products or services, close deals, or other miscellaneous purposes.

Make Clear and Concise Presentations

The essence of an effective presentation is to deliver with a simple but close-knit logical structure and a clear purpose, and to deliver a concise but strong message. Simplicity matters. One of the important skills of delivering a presentation is to speak in a way that's simple to follow. Different audiences have different understanding levels. Some audience may be familiar with the information you're delivering and even the jargon and technical terms; some may have little understanding. If your audience is not familiar with your topic or your field, you need to determine whether a concept that seems simple to you requires additional explanation. Use simple language. If the language is abstract and difficult, modify the language and tailor your presentation language directly to the audience's level of understanding to enhance the engagement.

Resonate and Interact with the Audience

To resonate and interact with your audience is a secret to successful delivery. To deliver engaging presentations, you need to connect with the audience and engage your audience with well-constructed content; also anticipate their needs, and respond effectively, making them feel like they're part of the presentation. Furthermore, emotions move your audience. Your enthusiasm is an essential element of your delivery skills. Your passion for the presentation itself can be contagious and help to elicit emotion in the audience, producing an effective emotional appeal, thus involving your audience in your presentation. It is also necessary to maintain conversational style with appropriate speed and volume during delivery. The distance between you and the audience will be shortened and it will be easier to convey the message for effective communication.

Practice makes perfect. In order to speak to your audience confidently in a comfortable manner, you should get familiar with the presentation structure, major points and supporting data, and the slides you made by rehearsing again and again. Before the presentation, you should learn about your audience and their prior knowledge, keep them in mind throughout the entire duration of your presentation, and use your knowledge of your audience's characteristics to tailor the message to their needs and speak enthusiastically. These will help you to establish your connection with your audience. Group activities can be designed to avoid boredom if the presentation is long. When the listeners have questions, you should respond courteously.

Use Non-verbal Communication Appropriately

Both verbal and non-verbal communication contribute to effective delivery. A good presenter combines verbal and non-verbal communication efficiently to enhance audience engagement. Verbal communication is the process of delivering the message with words. Non-verbal communication is to deliver the message with eye contact, facial expressions, gestures, postures, and the tone of voice. And messages transmitted through non-verbal language will be very helpful for you to capture the attention of the audience.

Eye contact helps to build trust and credibility between you and your audience. Making proper eye contact conveys your interest in the audience as individuals and you can look at the audience from one side of the room to the other side, and from the front row to the last row to check the feedback of your audience and adjust your speed. No one should underestimate the importance of non-verbal communication in presentations. With the right non-verbal communication means, you can easily win them over. Moving around will reduce the distance and barriers between you and your audience and make it easier for them to concentrate on your presentation.

7.3.3 Concluding a Presentation Effectively

A poor ending undermines an otherwise successful presentation delivery while a powerful ending creates a memorable presentation with a long-lasting impression. Your audience will remember the beginning and the ending of your presentation most clearly and thus learning how to end with a powerful impression is as important as starting a presentation with a strong beginning.

Summarize and Call for Action

There are various options to end a presentation. You can summarize and reiterate the main points to ensure that your audience understands the main purpose of your presentation. You can repeat the core message mentioned in the introduction to emphasize the connection between the beginning and the ending of your presentation. You can present a call to action with strong action verbs. For example, if you want your audience to accept your proposal for investing a certain project, ask them to take action. An effective presentation delivery ends with guidance on the next steps for the audience. Powerful quotes, humorous words, personal stories, memorable statements are also unique choices to connect with your audience by evoking emotion and making the presentation delivery end with a powerful impact and further action.

Handle the Q&A Session

Most professional presentations will complete the presentation process with a short question and answer session, which is a positive way to connect more with the audience and strengthen the interaction. Questions are useful for a presenter to gather feedback from the audience and encourage engagement in the presentation. Allowing the audience to ask questions after the presentation helps to clarify and reinforce your message and the audience will not leave the presentation with doubts or misconceptions. A Q&A session handled lively and successfully is stimulating and engaging for the audience; however, a Q&A session handled poorly leaves the audience with a negative impression of the presenter's message. To end the presentation process with a successful Q&A session, you need to be well-prepared, and the more well-prepared you are, the more natural you will be.

To prepare for the Q&A session, you can list possible questions and develop a strategic plan for how to confront tough and challenging questions. Questions from the audience can be good and meaningful questions, or difficult and unnecessary questions designed to challenge or even disapprove of your point of view. No matter what questions the audience asks, it is critical to listen carefully and to respond specifically; furthermore, good preparation helps you to give the best answer to questions which you have anticipated and given considerable thought.

Questions are to be answered clearly and succinctly and answers should be logically connected to what has been said in the presentation. Repeat the question if necessary and make sure all the listeners have heard the question clearly before you give an answer and your answer should be addressed to all listeners. If you do not know the answer, admit it and make a promise that you will look for an answer. After you finish all questions, it would be polite to close your presentation with a summary of the questions and express gratitude to your audience. This will make it clear to your audience that your presentation is finished.

Exercises

1. **Prepare a persuasive presentation according to the following information.**
   - Purpose of the presentation: to persuade to go cycling along the coast daily in order to improve their health.
   - Central idea: regular cycling activities improve both mental and physical health.

2. **Prepare an informative presentation according to the following information.**
   - Purpose of the presentation: to inform citizens in Xiamen about cycling routes and facilities designed and constructed by Xiamen Municipal Government.
   - Central idea: infrastructure facilities supporting cycling activities are available in Xiamen.

3. **Suppose you are a civil engineer of a construction company, responsible for solving the water-leaking problem of a tunnel under construction and you are going to make a presentation to managers. Prepare the presentation according to the following information.**

   The first point points out that the water-leaking problem has three characteristics, the second point points out that there are three major causes of the problem, and the third point talks about the solutions to the problem.

4. **To practice the skills needed to connect with an unfamiliar audience, prepare a 5-to 7-minute oral presentation according to the following guidelines and use PPT slides to support your presentation delivery.**

   Guidance: You are a manager of a tea club and you are unfamiliar with newly recruited club members. Choose an interesting topic on tea culture which is unfamiliar to the majority of your audience who are new to your tea club.

Chapter 8
Writing for the Web

In a competitive world where website development services are remarkably transforming the business industry, one particular piece of online information may attract millions of viewers and lead to effective communication results. The importance of website design and development in shaping business should never be underestimated. And as the number and use of websites continue to grow at an amazing speed, the skills of writing for the web become a necessity for successful career development.

Web writing follows unique writing conventions because the usability and accessibility of the content are as important as the content itself and learning to write for the web is different from learning any other style of writing. To present and sell through web writing is a basic skill in the workplace and understanding how the potential web users access, scan, and read web pages will help you to design user-oriented websites with efficient information. You need to align your writing skills with web development.

In this chapter, you will learn about:

- differences between a web page and a website;
- major types of websites used in the workplace;
- processes of creating reader-centered web pages;
- skills in developing content-based web pages.

8.1 Differences Between a Web Page and a Website

To write for the web successfully, you will need to keep in mind the following issues:

- What is a web page?
- What is a website?
- What are the differences between a web page and a website?

8.1.1 Web Pages

A web page is a document, commonly written in HTML. HTML is the abbreviation of Hyper-Text Markup Language which is a kind of computer language specifying how a web page should be formatted. With the help of HTML, web page writers can specify fonts, colors, images, headings, and everything that they want to display on a page by using web browsers. A web browser is the application software used to access the internet. Microsoft Internet Explorer, Safari, 360, Google Chrome are some famous web browsers. Millions of web pages are being added every day. When you click a link provided by a search engine, you are accessing a web page that may contain text, graphics, videos, and hyperlinks to other web pages and files.

A web page, which is often used to provide information to viewers, can be accessed by entering a URL address into the viewers' address bars. A web page may also be used as a method to sell products or services to viewers. For example:

Figure 8.1　A screenshot of a web page—VooV Meeting

The following is another example:

Figure 8.2　A screenshot of a web page—ZOOM

8.1.2 Websites

Multiple web pages make up a website and a website contains different web pages which are linked together with hyperlinks. The following is the home page of the official website of Encyclopedia Britannica, which provides encyclopedic information services:

Figure 8.3　A screenshot of a web page—Britannica

The following is a web page of Tim Hortons' official website, which promotes the coffee business of this well-known Canadian coffee company:

Figure 8.4　A screenshot of a web page—Tim Hortons

8.2　Major Types of Websites Used in the Workplace

Websites serve many different purposes in the workplace. Today, billions of websites are available for internet browsing, competing for the share of the attention. To write for the web successfully in the workplace, you will need to keep in mind the following issues:

Chapter 8 Writing for the Web

- What types of popular websites are often used in the workplace?
- What kind of website caters to your working environment?
- How to choose the right type of website to support your career development?

The internet has become a necessity in our daily life and in the workplace. We communicate, work, entertain, do the shopping, pay bills, and even organize our lives via websites. There are different types of websites used in the workplace and each has its unique features and advantages.

8.2.1 E-commerce Websites

If you work for a company dealing with e-business for selling or purchasing goods or services online, you need to learn to write for e-commerce websites. An e-commerce website is a kind of website which allows you to create an online store to sell your products to the customers in a digital way. With an e-commerce store, products and services can be sold online and online payments are allowed.

E-commerce websites can be an expansion of a company or an organization. In the workplace, this kind of website is the kind you must create if you are building a website for your company or organization and intend to sell your goods or services online. For example, Tesla is a company producing all-electric vehicles, also clean energy generation and storage products. Tesla vehicles are produced at its factory in Fremont, California, and Gigafactory Shanghai. The website is established for Tesla to promote the company and sell its goods or services.

Figure 8.5 A screenshot of a web page—TESLA

Nowadays, most large brands and many smaller ones have e-commerce websites. Taobao, Amazon, Walmart, eBay, Target, Flipkart, Newegg, Overstock, Best Buy are some of the most popular e-commerce websites, creating big online stores for the business to sell products and services digitally to target consumers. The following are some examples:

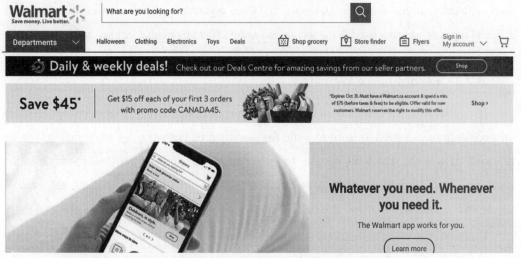

Figure 8.6　A screenshot of a web page—Walmart

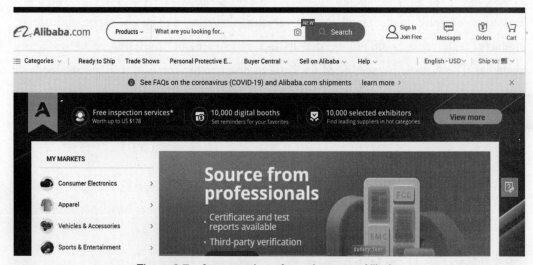

Figure 8.7　A screenshot of a web page—Alibaba

8.2.2 Corporate Websites

You need to learn to write for a corporate website if you work for a company or an organization. It is the most common one among the different types of websites and is the main representation of a company or an organization. A corporate website is an integral part of a larger marketing plan, providing a presence for a business, or offering news and advice about the world of business, finance, and entrepreneurship.

A corporate website is the closest to an e-commerce website; however, it is specifically devoted to promoting a company or an organization and not necessarily selling products or services. Most of the businesses today have websites reflecting good images, providing a range of services like banking, car rental, food ordering, and a variety of business services. Corporate websites are designed to present the identity regarding the company or organization, so are usually branded as the business in terms of the company logo, brand colors, and positioning.

The following are some examples of corporate websites owned by businesses to communicate with website visitors:

Figure 8.8 A screenshot of a web page—TOURISM AUSTRALIA

Figure 8.9　A screenshot of a web page—HUAWEI

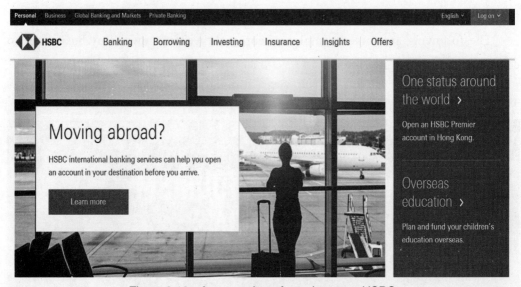

Figure 8.10　A screenshot of a web page—HSBC

8.2.3　Social Media Websites

Today, social networking websites have grown in numbers by leaps and bounds and have been important platforms for people to connect with colleagues, friends, or family members in the workplace or at home. Social media websites refer to websites and applications that are designed to allow people to share content quickly, efficiently, and broadly online. Social media websites encompass a wide range of websites and apps which allow users to share photos, opinions, and events broadly and engage with the public. And in the workplace, social media websites are used to help promote business.

For instance, Tencent QQ, WeChat, TikTok are some of the social media websites launched in China and got popular around the world. Tencent QQ, popularly known as QQ, is a chat-based social media platform for instant messaging. People can use QQ to stay in touch with friends through text messages, video calls, and voice chats. It has become international with more than 80 countries using it since it was launched in China. WeChat is also developed by Tencent and can easily work alongside QQ. It is an all-in-one communication app for messaging and calling and people use it to connect with other people around the world. Users can participate in group chats and send texts and audio or visual messages via WeChat. TikTok, which is known in China as Douyin, has become a massively popular social network around the world now. It is a social video app that allows its users to create various types of short videos for sharing.

Facebook, YouTube, Instagram, LinkedIn are some of the social media websites launched in the U.S. and got popular around the world. Facebook allows registered users to create profiles, upload photos and videos, send messages and keep in touch with friends, family, and colleagues. It allows users to post, read, and respond to classified ads, to find people who have common interests and interact with each other, to publicize an event, invite guests and track who plans to attend, to create and promote a public page built around a specific topic, to see which contacts are online and chat. YouTube is the world's largest video-sharing social networking site that enables users to upload and share videos. It enables users to create a YouTube channel to upload all their personally recorded videos to showcase to friends and followers. Instagram is launched as a unique social network website for users to upload photos and short videos, sharing the best moments of their life with family and friends.

In the age of digitalization, social media sites can take various forms and it is convenient for people to access social media websites through computers or smartphone apps. These sites are usually created to let people share thoughts, images or ideas, or simply connect with other people concerning a certain topic.

8.2.4 Educational Websites

Educational websites might also be geared towards fun learning for children or offer academic courses to adults. In the workplace, educational websites are popular because people tend to use this type of website to help themselves to transform careers with training, degrees, certificates in data science, computer science, and so on. The term "educational" covers a broad range of websites relating to education. The main goal of educational websites is to provide education to users and good educational websites are interactive and engaging for the users. Coursera and EdX are two famous educational websites. Coursera is an education platform that partners with top universities and organizations worldwide offer free online courses. Top universities like Yale, Michigan, Stanford, and leading companies like Google and IBM have joined Coursera to offer free courses for people around the world.

Figure 8.11　A screenshot of a web page—Coursera

EdX is a non-profit educational website created by founding partners Harvard and MIT to bring the best of higher education to students around the world. EdX offers MOOCs and interactive online classes in various subjects like law, history, engineering, business, computer science, public health, artificial intelligence (AI), and so on. Over 3,000 courses are offered by EdX.

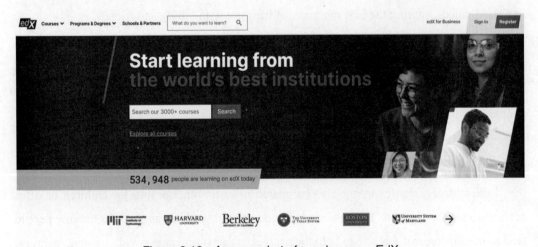

Figure 8.12　A screenshot of a web page—EdX

8.2.5 Personal Résumé Websites

Besides the up-mentioned websites which are often used in the workplace to keep the work moving on smoothly, there are personal websites designed to help you to get more career development opportunities. Today, recruiters are looking you up online, and a personal website that tells the story you want to tell can make all the difference between you and a competing candidate. A personal website can be customized and updated according to what you're working on, or what you want to emphasize. There are various types of personal websites, among which personal résumé websites and personal portfolios are typically useful ones.

The traditional résumé provides the basic background information of a job seeker, while a personal résumé website offers more detailed information. It can be used by all types of job seekers to share information and demonstrate technical skills and help job seekers to stand out among competitors. Even if you have very little work experience, you can create a website and build a better picture of your capabilities and yourself as a candidate.

The following is a web page of a personal résumé website designed by Bruce William who is a product designer:

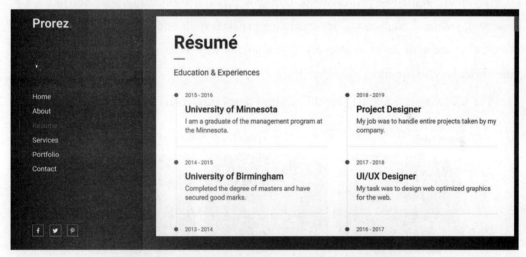

Figure 8.13　A screenshot of a web page—Bruce William

8.2.6 Personal Portfolio Websites

Personal portfolio websites have been most commonly employed by creative experts and freelancers to display and promote examples of previous works, attracting potential clients. It is a great way for writers, designers, filmmakers, artists and photographers, developers, and a wide range of artists to present their work online in the best possible manner and in a unique way to display their profile or talent to the world.

The following is a web page of the personal portfolio website established by Geraldine DeRuiter who is a writer and public speaker:

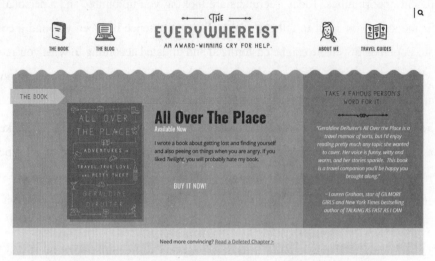

Figure 8.14　A screenshot of a web page—Geraldine DeRuiter

If you are skilled or professional, then you might use portfolio websites like a CV, presenting your professionalism, demonstrating personal skills and personal details to impress clients, customers, or future employers. It is a unique way to let others know about you and your personality, experience, and capabilities.

The following is a web page of the personal portfolio website of Stefanie Grieser:

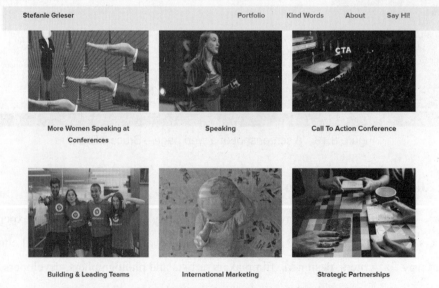

Figure 8.15　A screenshot of a web page—Stefanie Grieser

Chapter 8 Writing for the Web

8.3 Processes of Creating Reader-centered Web Pages

8.3.1 Analyzing Your Communication Purpose

When you create a web page, you are creating a platform to communicate with your potential readers. And you should be crystal clear about your potential readers and how to communicate with them successfully with your web writing skills. Interviews, surveys, and research of your targeted readers are necessary. Understanding your readers will help you to gather the information catering to the needs of your potential readers. After gathering the information, list the information logically so that your readers can locate the information efficiently with your assistance.

8.3.2 Planning and Designing Web Pages

Websites and web pages should be designed to be professional, attractive and engaging, and easy to navigate to quickly capture the attention and interest of the visitors. To help your readers to locate the information effectively, you need to plan a path for your readers so they can get connected with each web page from your home page with a practical menu. Your readers' needs, desires, and intuition are factors to be considered when you plan the path.

After you choose the structured framework, you can organize the visual elements and typography of a web page's design consistently within the interface. Besides planning the efficient path for your readers, you also need to understand the role of website grids so you can design attractive web pages. The website grid is a visual structure used to organize the content on the web page, and create alignment and order. Grids provide a common graphic language that makes it easier for you to create order among elements on a web page of a website. An effective website grid creates a good user experience and different website grids bring different user experiences. The following is a sketch of four widely used website grids for web pages:

Block grids are the simplest and they work well when presenting large continuous blocks of text or images. Column grids work well when the information being presented is discontinuous and different types of information can be placed in different columns. Modular grids work best for more complex problems where columns alone don't offer enough flexibility. Hierarchical grids can be used when none of the above grids will work to solve the problem.

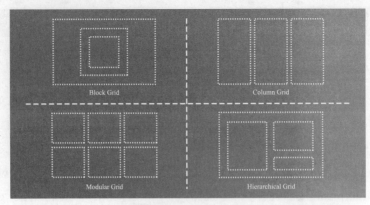

Figure 8.16　A sketch of four widely used website grids

8.3.3　Writing and Editing the Content

To create effective, powerful, and results-oriented web pages and make your website usable and attractive are two important targets when you design web pages. As you write content for your website pages, you need to think through how to write your website content, making sure the copy on each page serves its intended purpose, and end the page with a strong call to action.

To write content for a website, firstly you need to determine the purpose of the website. Only when you know the main purpose of the website clearly, will you be better positioned before writing to achieve that goal. Secondly, you need to research the audience and competing websites. Your visitors also visit websites of your competitors and researching competing websites inspires new content topics to write about to offer something unique, different, or better to your audience. Thirdly, you should have a plan for what pages you'll need and how all the web pages work together to display the content in varied ways. Then, you can begin to write content for the web pages and speak directly to the readers with clear and concise language. Finally, to draw the readers' eyes to important information, you can add page elements like images, buttons, icons, videos, charts and graphs, background colors, white space, line breaks, and so on.

Once you've finished writing the content of a web page, you need to revise and edit it to improve weak word choices, rewrite ambiguous sections, strengthen the headline, and check links to other content on your website. Then you can go back through each page and make sure you have used the main keyword naturally throughout the content to optimize your website content and guide both the web users and search engines to find your website. It's also important to keep your site content fresh, and you need to update the content and create versions of your page with different variations of headlines, calls to action, background colors, images, and so on to draw the readers' attention.

8.4 Skills in Developing Content-based Web Pages

A website is a group of web pages that share a domain and offers the best chance to make a great impression on potential customers online. The initial exposure helps website visitors to determine whether they want to spend more time reading, listening, or viewing. To avoid losing potential customers, strong content must be developed to cater to the needs of the visitors. To develop strong content successfully, you will need to keep in mind the following issues:

- What are the basic pages that should be included on your website?
- What are the functions of these basic pages?
- How to make the content of web pages strong and efficient?
- What skills are needed in developing a content-based web page?

The most common web pages on a website are the home page, about page, products or services page, and contact page.

A home page is the name of the main page of a website where visitors can find hyperlinks to other pages and usually serves as the starting point of a website. It is the first impression of the business on potential customers, guiding the visitors to their next step, or the call to action. The content of a home page is of great importance because it determines if an individual customer will browse around or say goodbye. An about page elaborates on the vision and accomplishments of your company or organization, and it usually includes brief company history, mission or vision statements, executive leadership information, and a few impactful client testimonials. The about page helps your company or organization to connect emotionally with potential customers. The products or services page is the crux of most websites. You need to tell visitors exactly whether you're selling products or services and enough information should be included for potential customers to understand the benefits of your products or services. Furthermore, you should ensure there is a clear call to action for next steps if a potential customer is interested in your products or services, whether it's to "buy now" or contact you for more information. The contact page is used as a customer support tool, directing customers to the right person or department so both parties can benefit. Any effective website contact page usually includes basic contact information like the company name, address, phone number, email address, etc. The contact page is extremely important because if visitors are on this page, they're trying to speak with you or ask some critical questions.

8.4.1 Creating Effective Content for Users

Content is the core of building positive relationships with users and creating effective content for users is the essential purpose of web writing. The quality and quantity of the content are one of the deciding factors when you predict the future success of a website. To develop the website and content effectively and to improve user engagement, you need to analyze how people seek out and understand your content and plan the content with usability and attractiveness in mind.

In web design, usability refers to how easy a website is for visitors to find what they need. Usability is the major concern of website readers. Most website readers go to a website to find specific information or service. It is of vital importance to help your readers to locate what they want quickly and efficiently, or the readers may abandon your website and turn to other websites for what they want. Even if you have successfully created high-quality web content, you still need to update the content in time to ensure that the potential customers find it effortless and beneficial to use the website.

Attractiveness is the other essential factor in website design. Some visitors are just browsing. They're curious about what's on your site, happy to move from link to link as long as they find content that interests them. When they lose interest, they will quit and shift to another site. So to keep viewers (who may be customers or future customers), your website has to make finding specific information easy and provide a pleasant experience for those who are just browsing. Ultimately, finding this balance comes down to being reader-friendly, writing well, and using AIDA. Get browsers' attention, keep their interest, create desire for your products or services, and get action if you can.

8.4.2 Writing Web Pages with Clarity and Conciseness

When you are writing web pages for your company or organization, you are a web page writer. In order to keep your web users interested in your content, you must find a way to keep your web content clear, concise, and significant. Writing web content is rarely a simple task for a web page writer because web content needs to be accessible to anyone who happens to land on the web page. To write effective and efficient web content, web page writers should write the content with clarity and conciseness in mind.

To enhance clarity, you need to place the most important information at the beginning of a web page. Web writing demands a unique structure catering to web users' needs. Users usually begin at the top of your page, reading across to determine what products, services, or information you are providing. Using eye-catching headings and subheadings will show your products and services directly and clearly to web users. Starting with a conclusion by presenting the most important information first on each content page will provide web users with greater detail as they scroll down the page. Organizing the content hierarchically from the general to the specific will make the structure of the text clear and logical.

Web pages must be concise because web users don't read the content word for word; instead, they scan pages for the information they need. Short and to-the-point paragraphs are better than long and complicated ones. Bulleted and numbered lists are often used with a concise explanation instead of narrative text, helping users to locate the information efficiently. It's an important skill for web page writers to write with precise language and short, succinct sentences because web users are more than willing to walk away from long, rambling content that lacks a point or definite direction. Clear and concise language helps reinforce the credibility of your website and make the content as professional as possible. All websites are informative and designed for certain purposes. Writing for websites clearly and effectively helps you and your company or organization to get more opportunities.

❯ Exercise

Study the following web page and answer the following questions. For each question, there are four choices marked A, B, C and D. Choose the best answer.

1) What kind of grid is used in the following web page?

    A. The block grid.   B. The column grid.

    C. The modular grid.   D. The hierarchical grid.

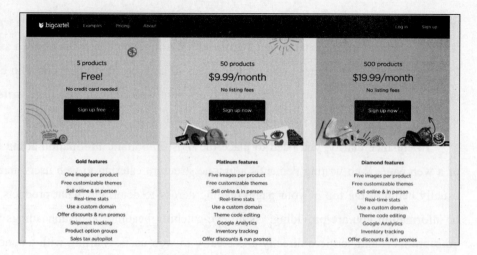

2) Which type of coffee creamer cannot be found on the following e-commerce web page?

A. Liquid creamer. B. Sweetened dairy creamer.

C. Powdered creamer. D. Non-dairy creamer.

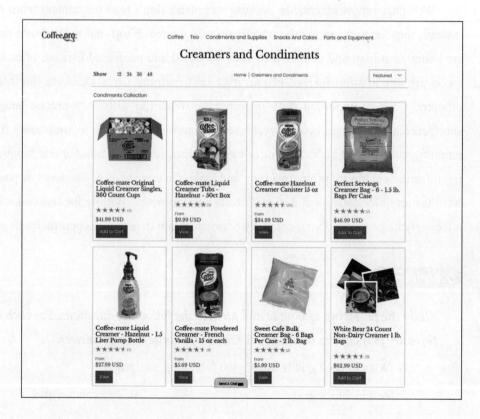

Chapter 8 Writing for the Web

3) Which organization does MOA belong to?

A. River Ironeagle-Mindel.

B. Curator of UBC.

C. University of British Columbia.

D. National Youth Organization.

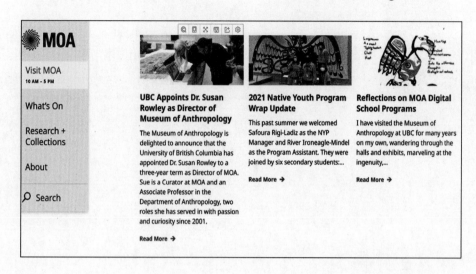

References

Anon. 2021a. Bad News Letter. *UCSB*. Retrieved March 19, 2021, from UCSB website.

Anon. 2021b. Block Letter Format. *ABT*. Retrieved October 28, 2021, from ABT website.

Anon. 2021c. Building Confidence in COVID-19 Vaccines Among Your Patients: Tips for the Healthcare Team. *CDC*. Retrieved February 12, 2021, from CDC website.

Anon. 2021d. Michigan Department of Education Memo. *Michigan Department of Education*. Retrieved April 16, 2021, from Michigan Department of Education website.

Anon. 2021e. Proposal Letter—For a Joint Education Program. *Writinghelp-central*. Retrieved July 27, 2021, from Writinghelp-central website.

Anon. 2021f. Resume Examples. *Ginger Software*. Retrieved August 21, 2021, from Ginger Software website.

Anon. 2021g. Writing Persuasive Messages. *Docshare*. Retrieved June 10, 2021, from Docshare website.

Bailey, E. P. 1996. *Plain English at Work: A Guide to Writing and Speaking*. New York: Oxford University Press.

Bailey, E. P. 1997. *The Plain English Approach to Business Writing*. Oxford: Oxford University Press.

Bailey, E. P. 2014. *Writing & Speaking at Work*. New York: Pearson.

Barrass, R. 2002. *Writing at Work: A Guide to Better Writing Administration, Business and Management*. London: Routledge.

Bennett, S. 2014. *The Elements of Resume Style*. New York: Amacom.

Bernhardt, S. A. & Smith, E. L. 1996. *Writing at Work: Professional Writing Skills for People on the Job*. Lincolnwood: NTC Pub Group.

Campanizzi, J. 2005. *Effective Writing for the Quality Professional*. Milwaukee: ASQ Quality Press.

Chesla, E. L. 1997. *Improve Your Writing for Work*. New York: LearningExpress.

Davis, K. 2010. *Business Writing and Communication*. New York: McGraw-Hill Education.

Doyle, A. 2021. How to Format a Professional Email Message. *The Balance Careers*. Retrieved May 15, 2021, from The Balance Careers website.

Forbus, R. & Snyder, J. L. 2014. *Today's Business Communication: A How-to Guide for the Modern Professional*. New York: Business Expert Press.

Gillis, O. 2021. 6 Rules of Thumb for Creating Website Grids. *Elementor*. Retrieved September 18, 2021, from Elementor website.

Grieser, S. 2021. Hello! I'm Stef. *Stefaniegrieser*. Retrieved August 29, 2021, from Stefaniegrieser website.

Hobbs, B. 2021. Example of a Good News Memo. *Term Paper Warehouse*. Retrieved May 14, 2021, from Term Paper Warehouse website.

Hood, J. H. 2013. *How to Book of Writing Skills*. New York: WordCraft Global Pty.

Keiling, H. 2021. Functional Resume: Definition, Tips and Examples. *Indeed*. Retrieved November 13, 2021, from Indeed website.

Kirschman, D. 2002. *Getting Down to Business: Successful Writing at Work*. New York: LearningExpress.

Kolin, P. C. 2016. *Successful Writing at Work*. Belmont: Wadsworth Publishing.

Locker, K. O. & Kienzler, D. S. 2015. *Business and Administrative Communication*. New York: McGraw-Hill Education.

Mackey, D. 2005. *Send Me a Message: A Step-by-step Approach to Business and Professional Writing*. New York: McGraw-Hill Education.

Marison. 2022. Sales Letter for Travel Agency. *Lettersfree*. Retrieved May 1, 2022, from Lettersfree website.

Mizrahi, J. 2015. *Writing for the Workplace: Business Communication for Professionals*. New York: Business Expert Press.

Scott, G. & Slack, M. 2021. Cover Letter Examples for All Job Applications. *Resume Genius*. Retrieved September 24, 2021, from Resume Genius website.

Tomaszewski, M. 2021. Combination Resume (Template & 5+ Combo Examples). *Zety*. Retrieved October 23, 2021, from Zety website.

Young, D. J. 2008. *Business English: Writing in the Global Workplace*. New York: McGraw-Hill Education.

Keys to Exercises

Chapter 1

Extract 1

Comments:

1) Simplicity. The writer seems to have tried to make a simple subject unnecessarily complex.

2) Clarity. The meaning is not clear. Is it that (replacing 78 words with 18): a driver should always be able to stop within the distance that can be seen to be clear?

Extract 2

Comments:

1) Appropriateness. Long words are used although short words would have served the writer's purpose better.

2) Brevity. More words are used than are needed to convey a simple message. What is said in 75 words could have been said clearly and simply, more forcefully, and more persuasively, in 41:

Learning by trial and error wastes time and does not necessarily lead to a satisfactory outcome. For example, some who type with two fingers may appear to type quickly but do not work as fast or as accurately as competent touch-typists.

Chapter 2

1. 1) The entrance exam was failed by one-third of the applicants.

—Not clear or concise. Use an active rather than a passive verb.

Revised:

One-third of the applicants failed the entrance exam.

2) Children under 12 years old cannot participate in the competition.

—Not constructive.

Revised:

Children over 12 years old can participate in the competition.

3) We are pleased to inform you that we have selected you for an interview for the executive secretary position.

—Not courteous. Writing should be "you"-centered.

Revised:

You have been selected to be interviewed for the executive secretary position.

4) He distributed annual reports to the recipients bound in white and blue covers.

—Not clear. The misplaced modifier creates an incorrect if humorous picture—of the recipients wrapped in white and blue covers.

Revised:

He distributed to the audience annual reports bound in white and blue covers.

5) A new photocopier is needed by the employees in the Foreign Affairs Division.

—Not clear or concise. Use an active verb.

Revised:

The Foreign Affairs Division employees need a new photocopier.

2. **In the past month** [showing time], our company's sales have gone down 30%. **As a result** [causation], our cash flow situation has become critical. **Worse** [contrast], this loss of revenue could even threaten our company's future. **Therefore** [causation], we need to take action to prevent bankruptcy, **including** [illustration] working harder to get sales and cutting our production costs.

3. 1) Vague   2) Clear   3) Vague   4) Clear   5) Vague   6) Clear

Chapter 3

1) **Correct version:**

The most important things in life are:

- being happy [The original item is not parallel; the noun is revised here to a participle.]
- having good friends
- making a good income. [We suggest a period at the end of the list.]

Keys to Exercises

If the items in the indented list are not full sentences, don't capitalize the initial letter of the beginning word.

Another correct version:

The most important things in life are

- happiness,
- good friends, and [Parallel nouns (with appropriate adjectives and articles).]
- a good income. [A period at the end of the list; appropriate punctuation throughout.]

2) **Correct version:**

When you assemble a desk, be sure to do the following: [Full sentences take colons.]

- Make sure all parts are in the box; [Punctuation could be a comma, too.]
- Use the correct tools; [Punctuation could be a comma, too.]
- Keep your temper. [A period at the end of the list needed for consistency.]

3) **Correct version:**

My favorite novels are:

- *Wuthering Heights*
- *Vanity Fair*
- *Tess of the D'Urbervilles*. [Novel titles should be in italics; we should follow grammatical conventions in lists; we suggest a period at the end of the list.]

Chapter 4

1.

Li Xiaoming Assistant Professor	**Summary** Insightful Assistant Professor with three years of classroom expertise. Expert in language teaching and the content-based teaching method with a commitment to long-term student success. Proven history of helping both students and professors to achieve academic goals.
Contact Information Address Room 221, No.6 Zhongshan Road, Guangzhou, Guangdong Province, PRC 100021 Phone 13600022166	
	Work History September 2019–Present XXX Foreign Studies University, Zhanjiang, Guangdong • Assisted professors and school administrators with continuous development, review, planning, and outcome

Email 13600022166@163.com **Skills** Academic research Class instruction **Languages** Japanese French	evaluation to measure language program performance. • Contributed to planning appropriate and engaging lessons for both classroom and distance learning applications. • Evaluated and supervised student activities and performance levels to provide reports on academic programs. • Used a variety of learning modality and support materials to facilitate the learning process and presentations, including visual, aural, and social learning modality.
Education	
September 2014– July 2019	Ph.D.: Applied Linguistics Central South University, 982 Lushan Road, Changsha, Hunan Province, PRC 410012
September 2010– July 2014	Master of Arts: English Language and Literature Central South University, 982 Lushan Road, Changsha, Hunan Province, PRC 410012
Accomplishments • Collaborated with a team of language teaching in the development of e-learning language software which supported over 2,000 students during the online teaching period in 2020.	
References References are available upon request.	

2.–3. Omitted

Chapter 5

1.

Dear Sir or Madam,

The real estate market in the West Coast province has witnessed a sudden interest in residential properties. Buyers are constantly on the lookout for real estate developers who will not only showcase their properties but also guide them in making the right choices.

Crankstein and Crick is one such leading real estate developer, offering a host of properties to choose from in the area. Our properties include residential apartments and condos in the residential space, as well as commercial properties. While our properties deliver excellence in architectural design and quality standards, we also assist customers in making an informed choice depending on their budget and lifestyle. Our corporate tagline, "Look no further", is intended to provide a one-stop shop for prospective buyers who need to be assisted throughout the prospecting and purchase process.

The latest in our bouquet of offerings is our child-centric homes designed to ensure the safety and security of children. With electrical connections out of a small child's reach, elevators and doorbells that can be easily reached by children, CCTV cameras within play areas, and separate driveways for vehicles at a clear distance from a child's promenade area, these amenities are sought after by families who value safety.

We would be delighted if you visit our site office at 22 Norfox Street on any day between 11:00 a.m. and 6:00 p.m. for a guided tour of our facilities. We're looking forward to being of assistance and assure you of our valued service.

Yours sincerely,

Alex

2.

Dear Customers,

We are pleased to announce the opening of our new branch of outlets in the city

(Continued)

downtown on January 10, 2021. The opening of the new branch is part of our continuous efforts to provide the best shopping experience to all of our clients in Xiamen.

We are also happy to announce a 40% discount on selected items from January 10 to January 18 in all of our outlets to mark off the start of the new holiday season.

We would like to thank you all for your loyalty and support. We could not have made it throughout the years without your continuous support. We value each one of our customers and will do our best to provide the best service all the time.

Sincerely,

John Davis

3.
194 Greenland Road, Haichang

Xiamen, Fujian Province

China 360000

Phone: (0592) 111–2221

Email: Elizabethlee@xmut.org

August 10, 2021

Ms. Molly Ladner

Head of Office

Visa and Immigration Office

Canadian Embassy Beijing

19 Dongzhimenwai Dajie

Chaoyang District

Beijing, PRC 100600

Dear Ms. Ladner,

Thank you for your writing for further information on the visa application process. Your

Keys to Exercises

(Continued)

further support will be appreciated.

I am a professor of the Faculty of International Languages, AAA University of Technology, a young and dynamic university established by the local government and is now located in Haichang, Xiamen. I was selected by my university and University of BBB in Canada to be the international visiting scholar for two years from September 1, 2021 to September 1, 2023 on the basis of joint cooperation between the two universities. My university will give me full financial support for all my expenses on research, travel expenses from China to Canada and from Canada to China, accommodation, food, books, and supplies at University of BBB.

According to the invitation letter from University of BBB, an entry visa and work permit authorized by you will be needed. I have prepared all materials required by Visa and Immigration Office, Canadian Embassy Beijing for application of Temporary Resident Visa and Work Permit at your convenience.

Thank you for your attention! Should you wish to call me, the number is (0592) 111–2221 and my email address is Elizabethlee@xmut.org.

Sincerely yours,

Elizabeth Lee

4. **Subject Line:** A Discount Coupon for You

Dear Sir/Madam,

Thank you so much for being a customer of Sunshine Shopping Mall.

It's because of the support of clients like you that we have been able to be in business for such a long time. To thank you for your support, we have prepared a discount coupon especially for you.

(Continued)

> Please see the attachment for electronic coupons. You can download the coupons to your cell phone for future shopping. Each coupon has a unique code number, and you may show the code to our cashier to get a discount of 30% from any product in our store or our online store.
>
> The offer is only available for the first 300 customers who make the purchase before June 20, 2022.
>
> Yours sincerely,
>
> Linda Fleck

Chapter 6

1.
> **Terrapin Marmot Figurines, Ltd.**
>
> 2334 South Ripley Road, Terrapin, TX, 79555
>
> **To:** Bill Cleary, Financial Manager
> **From:** Penelope Anderson, General Manager
> **Date:** January 24, 2019
> **Subject:** Terrapin Marmot Figurines Investment in Rockwallen Funds
>
> Text goes here.
>
> PA/lk
>
> Enclosure: Financial figures for the fourth quarter
> cc: Natalie Henstrick, President

2.–3. Omitted

Chapter 7

1.–4. Omitted

Chapter 8

1) B   2) B   3) C